Self

Síreacht: Longings for Another Ireland is a series of short, topical and provocative texts on controversial issues in contemporary Ireland.

Contributors to the *Síreacht* series come from diverse backgrounds and perspectives but share a commitment to the exposition of what may often be disparaged as utopian ideas, minority perspectives on society, polity and environment, or critiques of received wisdom. Associated with the phrase *ceól sírechtach síde* found in Irish medieval poetry, *síreacht* refers to yearnings such as those evoked by the music of the *aos sí*, the supernatural people of Irish mythology. As the title for this series, we use it to signify longings for and imaginings of a better world in the spirit of the World Social Forums that 'another world is possible'. At the heart of the mythology of the *sí* is the belief that lying beneath this world is the other world. So too these texts address the urgent challenge to imagine potential new societies and relationships, but also to recognise the seeds of these other worlds in what already exists.

Other published titles in the series are

Freedom? by Two Fuse
Public Sphere by Harry Browne
Commemoration by Heather Laird
Money by Conor McCabe

The editors of the series, Órla O'Donovan, Fiona Dukelow and Rosie Meade, School of Applied Social Studies, and Heather Laird of the School of English, University College Cork, welcome suggestions or proposals for consideration as future titles in the series. Please see http://sireacht.ie/ for more information.

Self

EILÍS WARD

CORK UNIVERSITY PRESS

First published in 2021 by
Cork University Press
Boole Library
University College Cork
T12 ND89
Ireland

Library of Congress Control Number: 2021939153

British Library Cataloguing in Publication Data
A CIP catalogue record for this book is available from the British
Library.

ISBN - 9781782054870

Typeset by Studio 10 Design
Printed by Gutenberg Press in Malta

Cover image: © Shutterstock.com

www.corkuniversitypress.com

CONTENTS

*This book is dedicated, with a deep bow
of gratitude, to Alain Liebmann and
Paul Haller, two great teachers.*

ACKNOWLEDGEMENTS

This book was nudged along, shaped and refined through many conversations with many people, some sustained and some random. For this I would like to thank Brendan Breen, Colin Brown, Andrew Collins, Fintan Coughlan, Peter Doran, Mary Flanagan, Mary McGill, Connie Masterson, Linda O'Nolan, Peter Rocca, Maeve Taylor and Gillian Wylie. Thanks to a Bodhisattva of technology, Gareth McElhinney, for not flinching, and to Shuho Catherine Spaeth, who allowed me to use her beautiful poem, which I first heard in Tassajara Zen Mountain Centre in early 2020. Thank you also to Rosie Meade and her three co-editors at *Síreacht* for very helpful comments along the way. I would also like to thank Derrydonnell Woods for providing shelter and inspiration. Finally, thanks also to the students of the NUIG BA module that I taught over many years, 'Buddhism, Politics, Society', whose enthusiasm for Buddhist ideas and for contemplative education eased the path greatly. I am the only one responsible for the content and conclusions drawn.

Standing together on the road
in the deep silence of snowy mountains
binding the self without a rope
one bright pearl.

SHUHO CATHERINE SPAETH

Introduction

Sketching the Field: Neoliberalism, Buddhism and the Self

For a time, it seemed like this book might be derailed by the coronavirus. As we were all forced into narrow domesticated relationships and a stripped-back life, the necessity of community and the social contract were laid bare to us. In the early weeks of our first lockdown, we responded with bountiful acts of generosity and kindness to each other, including, most especially, to those we did not even know. Not only did we rush to support individuals cocooning around us and to donate money to provide our healthcare workers with hot, nourishing food in hospitals, but we also welcomed and valued the state's role as provider and container of our lives. We accepted diminutions of our freedoms in the interest of public health. We felt and deeply appreciated the sense of collective belonging and collective effort that sprang up seemingly naturally.

Since the early flush and notwithstanding the continued uncertainty of outcomes, it is clear also that it will be business as usual in some regards. Or perhaps to put it differently, the coronavirus has accelerated trends that were already under way, including the kind of trends treated in this book. One trend is the continued elevation of the individual, isolated self as the core of our understanding of what it means to be a human today. If the social distancing required produced what musician and performer Iarla Ó Lionáird poetically called 'super solitary spaces', then that solitariness, or some version of it, may remain with us for some time.[1] That acceleration is partly a perverse outcome brought on by the ongoing requirement for us to remain distant from each other and the concomitant loss of much of the social world in which we make meaning for ourselves. It is also intentional, such as the inevitable institutionalisation of home-working as the norm, thus depriving us of the critical social connections that workplaces provide. As Ó Lionáird said, many experienced the withdrawal from social and cultural activities as a withdrawal from what it is that makes us human. Covid-19 too deprived us of much of the everyday human touch and intimacy that is equally important to our sense of being human.

In time then, while considering this book's place in a post-Covid landscape, I came to see the Covid world as capturing most dramatically the kind of tension treated in the book. One the one hand, we need each other (as we discovered again during our lockdown months), and on the other hand, the neoliberal era has actually rendered us potentially toxic to each other, and to ourselves, symbolised and manifest in our vulnerability to an invisible chain of proteins that has the capacity to cause havoc in our bodies and to kill. While we do not know the precise source of Covid-19, it is likely to have emerged as a result of human actions (such as environmental ruptures or industrial-scale animal husbandry) and its spread has been facilitated by a world in which containment of travel and movement of goods and services has all but gone. It is almost as if, as some authors quoted in this book suggest, neoliberalism has the potential to destroy the very conditions that it has necessarily created and, in so doing, take down human civilisation also.

The idea for this book, however, was sparked by a much simpler scenario: a conversation I had on a very gloomy February afternoon some years ago with a young graduate student in my office in the university in Galway. I asked about her future plans and, in response, hesitatingly, she told me about an evening recently spent with a group of her former college friends, all young like herself and, I thought, probably also confident, bright, energetic and talented. What she told me stopped me in my tracks. It brought into the room the darker side of our current condition in all its destructive tensions and impossible demands. It revealed the extent of the crippling harm being done to younger people.

She told me that her friends had tentatively come

around to confessing their deep feelings of hopelessness about their futures. None of them was likely to become a start-up entrepreneur in business or technology. None had founded an NGO nor achieved fame and public admiration for efforts on behalf of animals or the environment. None showed promise as social entrepreneurs. Consequently, they were floundering and found it hard not to be depressed. They felt that they were *already* social and personal failures.

The startling tale revealed to me the core of our current neoliberal order and its deeply corrosive impact. So ubiquitous as to be virtually invisible, neoliberalism has come to shape not only our economies and our public spaces, but also our understanding of what it means to be human. I could not shrug the story off as simply a version of young people's historically constant struggle to make their way in the world past the shelter of family and education. What struck me was not just the feelings of despair, but that the model of the 'entrepreneur' was the standard against which everything about their lives was measured and that these young adults had internalised its specific values about success and failure. Accordingly, they were failures before their adult lives had properly begun.

In this book I want to interrogate the consequences of neoliberal values for what it means to be human at this stage of the twenty-first century. I want to do it, moreover, by suggesting that a Buddhist account of the self offers both a profound critique of neoliberal subjectivity and an alternative to it that is more in tune with how we actually are in the world and with what we need to do to rescue ourselves from neoliberalism's 'deceitful' emancipatory claims that force us to embrace our servitude as though it were our liberation.[2]

Thus, two big sets of ideas structure this book, neoliberalism and Buddhism, and coming close behind is a third big idea, what I have learned to call therapy culture. For all three big ideas, I draw in voices of experts and critics and thus present language and concepts used in their work. The mode of enquiry throughout the book is both academic and personal, reflecting two kinds of curiosity: my scholarly curiosity about how and why this new person has come into life, and my personal, Buddhist-inflected curiosity about how the true nature of being can be rescued from its deceit. While the former reaches to interrogate concepts, the latter strives to remain rooted in the day-to-day experience of being human in order to do the work of reducing human suffering. Both, I suggest, are needed. We need to both fully grasp neoliberalism's power to prescribe and shape what it means to be human, and find an alternative ground that is itself nourishing of the human spirit. In the chapters that follow, I will weave these ideas and approaches together to make my case. First, though, it may be helpful to set out some broad understandings of neoliberalism and the context for the use of Buddhist thought.

What is neoliberalism? Neoliberalism is not merely the latest stage of capitalism, instead it contains something radical: its reshaping of our sense of self. Neoliberalism emerged after the Second World War, initially from two groups of economists, one attached to the University of Chicago and the other in Germany, at the centre of which was Friedrich Hayek. Hayek proposed that all human activity is a form of economic calculation and should therefore be governed by the rules of market exchange. The 'laws' of supply and demand constituted the only way to allocate resources, and their full efficiency could be achieved only when markets were freed up from all external interference, such as from governments. According to this view, free-market economies were not in fact *part of* society but, in their expansion into all realms of human activity, *became* society.[3]

Famously, these ideas made their way into the political visions of British prime minister Margaret Thatcher and US president Ronald Reagan, in the 1970s and '80s. As a loyal Hayek fan, Mrs Thatcher sought to marry his proposals with Conservative Party norms about family life and hard work, exemplified in her much-quoted statement that there is 'no such thing as society'. The collapse of the former Soviet Union, provider of an alternative vision and political resistance to capitalism's onward march, freed up the pitch for neoliberalism to move to a position of global hegemony, and by the early decades of the new century, neoliberalism *was* the new global reality.

Neoliberalism's defining characteristics can be sum-marised as, first, a deregulation of economies; second, a forcing open of national markets to international trade and capital; and third, a shrinking of the state's realm through privatisation, austerity, or both. Hence, neo-liberalism is often seen as a macro-economic framework, grounded on the presupposition that 'the markets' are unimprovable and they are often spoken about as though they are some natural and quasi-sacred force. But the trick of neoliberalism is that it doesn't just concern economics. Instead, there is an economisation of all realms, including those where no money transactions are involved. Everything is governed by the laws of supply and demand, to which, in turn, supreme authority is granted. It plays out, for instance, in how schools are rated and then chosen by parents and in how we manage ourselves on dating websites. The radicalism of its shift is that it has reordered our social reality through its defining belief that competition is the only legitimate organising principle for human activity. In this, critically, it is a break with the contract between the citizen and the state that constitutes the traditional basis of western liberal democracies. Neoliberalism does not argue that the state and its institutions – such as elected governments – are not needed. Rather, the state's role will be much reduced: to manage disputes, promote competition and, not least, produce a certain kind of subject who conducts herself in a certain way. This new subject is the fluid, risk-taking, resilient, competitive individual who no longer sees herself as part of a collective or of 'society' but prioritises and internalises her individual enhancement. In the neoliberal world, 'society' becomes an enterprise itself made up of enterprises, or of individuals competing with each other as enterprises, competing for resources and for better outcomes, be it financial success, happiness, or perfection of the thing we have learned to call a 'lifestyle'.

Neoliberalism's lodestar is that *all* human conduct is economic conduct.[4] Its configuration of all aspects of existence in economic terms is such that persons too are expected to comport themselves as if they are corporations. The term *homo economicus* has been used to describe this new person, the necessary handmaid of neoliberal economics. As we will see, however, she comes endowed with a naturalness and legitimacy so deeply burrowed into our everyday language, practices and consciousness that it is difficult to discern another way of being. Neoliberalism's seductive power is partially built on the fact that there is no single part of the neoliberal self that we do not already recognise within ourselves.

It is possible to think about neoliberalism from the perspective of its destruction of our ecosystems or its deepening of inequalities. But this book's focus is specifically on its ontology, or its understanding of and impact on what it means to be human. At its centre is an argument that the neoliberal self is a being stripped to become an entity without, or that comes before, the social. Her sense of self is evacuated of the social. I have no quarrel with Korean philosopher Byung-Chul Han's view that neoliberalism contains a 'diabolical logic'. By this he means its fragmentation of humans and elimination of solidarity in accordance with its supreme myth – internalised by us – that human freedom is found in autonomy from the other and in the totalisation of production.[5]

And why Buddhist thought? Its popular imagery of calmness and inscrutability does not at first glance suggest tools for critique. My case is that Buddhist thought provides both a ground for critique of neoliberalism and an alternative to its conceptualisation of a self. It allows us to think in a comprehensive way about the jeopardy of neoliberalism precisely because it holds up a very different view of what it means to be human: that is, that we are thoroughly, necessarily and irreducibly social. However, as I will discuss in the fifth chapter, Buddhist thought too has been enlisted, though in a misplaced fashion, to work towards our current servitude.

Buddhist thought has been brought into this book, however, largely because of my personal interest as a practitioner of (Soto) Zen Buddhism. I first began practising Zen in the early 1990s with an Irish-based French Zen priest who had been a student of a Japanese Zen teacher. More recently, I affiliated myself with the San Francisco Zen Centre and became immersed in what is sometimes classified as 'American Zen'. It was here, in particular, that I found an expression of Buddhism which allowed me to integrate the secularised, contemporary life that I live as an Irish citizen, in a particular place and time, and which also folded in with my socialist, feminist and environmentalist values.

Buddhist thought draws on a view of the human subject first articulated by the person known as the Buddha in the preliterate Iron Age in India over 2,500 years ago. These ideas made their way across continents from India, to China and Japan and, in time, to the West, in each place being changed somewhat by local culture and values. My focus, however, will be on contemporary accounts predominantly from a Zen perspective. My task is made easier by the recent flourishing of dialogue between Buddhist thought and western psychology such as that arising from a shared account of what it means to be human. Western psychology contains a view of the self as a biopsychosocial being, a dynamic product of interactions between our biology (our genetic inheritance), our psychological inheritance (childhood relationships, especially those of early childhood) and the wider social and political environment. Within this account, our genetic inheritance remains largely invariable, our childhood experiences remain profound, and the social environment does play a significant role in how we think and feel about ourselves and act in the world.[6] This power that the 'outside world' has, to inscribe on our bodies, our sense of self and our identity, is now a commonplace idea in psychological thinking, such that identity is often conceived of as a 'becoming' rather than a 'being'.[7] In this alone, much is shared with Buddhism.

To proceed with this book's enquiry, I present in the first chapter the internal architecture or the psyche of the neoliberal subject. In the next chapter, I go on to refine this content to draw in the relationship between neoliberalism and what is sometimes referred to as a 'pandemic' of mental ill health today, and the relationship of both to what has been called 'therapy culture'. In the third chapter, I present a Buddhist account of the self, and in the fourth, present some further refinement, in this case on the necessity of the social to the self in Buddhism. Here I draw on a research project I undertook on Buddhist peace work in Cambodia. In the fifth chapter, I turn my attention to the question of mindfulness, not only because this is a Buddhist-inflected idea that has taken up residency in our psyches and in society in recent decades, and is therefore of interest, but largely because, as I argue, it has a complicated relationship with neoliberalism. I make the case that a version of mindfulness has become part of the problem. My final chapter draws on all of these themes to conclude that Buddhist thought offers us both a profound and liberating challenge to neoliberal subjectivity and an alternative vision of an ethical life, one which embraces our very interdependency as the ground on which we can live well together, sentient and nonsentient beings.

What is the
Neoliberal Self?

Over thirty years ago, sociologist Nikolas Rose began to notice changes in how people understood themselves. It was expressed directly in their language and behaviour and in how they talked about their personal feelings, their secret hopes and ambitions and their disappointments. It showed up in their interactions with their bosses and workmates, with their partners, children and friends. Its comprehensiveness was such that he felt some kind of revolution had occurred. It was, he said, revolutionary because of its ontological implications, or its implications for what it means to be human. People were speaking about themselves as if they were a 'project' to be worked on, in the same way that capital or resources are managed, and acting accordingly. They saw themselves as enterprises in a great sea of enterprises and understood that their purpose was to maximise the value of existence to the self.[8]

The change was not sudden but part of a slow, inexorable process and, thirty years on, Rose's diagnosis now seems extraordinarily prescient. It has become a lot clearer that the 'out there' of neoliberalism both requires and produces an equivalent 'in here' found in this new kind of subject. By all appearances, this new subject seems to have fulfilled Margaret Thatcher's desire to change people's 'souls', and it manifests her much-quoted belief that there is, in fact, no such thing as 'society'. This neoliberal self, whether found in the ideal or playing out in a more fragmented way in how we value and think about ourselves, constitutes a very powerful and comprehensive mode of being for which economic reasoning is the defining rationale.[9]

This book argues that the neoliberal self, or the neoliberal subject, constitutes no less than a denial of what it means to be human. If neoliberal capitalism will destroy our civilisation,[10] its shaping of the human self is a crucial element of that destructive power. The neoliberal subject is, thus, not just an interesting cultural phenomenon or, as is sometimes stated, a highpoint of human achievement. I argue that it empties out what is at the very core of our selves. Neoliberalism seeks to tear up our profound interdependence, our shared ontology, or the very depth of the social within us that allows us to grow and flourish and to live emotionally and psychologically sustainable lives. In eliminating bonds of solidarity and relationality between us, it produces a fragmentation of ourselves as human beings. Moreover, expected to live more and more as good neoliberal subjects, we perversely deepen the disorders that threaten human life. This is neoliberalism's 'diabolical logic': the idea that the peak of human freedom is found in autonomy from others.[11] It is these ideas that I wish to present and tease out in this chapter.

One helpful way of thinking through these ideas is to conceive of neoliberalism as a layered set of social norms. Social norms set out behavioural rules for us to follow, a moral agenda that prescribes how things ought and ought not to be and, importantly, the sanctions that will result if there are deviations.[12] From childhood onwards, our behaviour is shaped by many social norms. We learn the etiquette around eating, for instance, and how to behave in public places. In school we are socialised into norms about waiting our turn, sharing, and communicating with others. Social norms function in ways that are often barely visible to us even as they do their work. They are often closely intertwined with dominant religious and cultural values so that they are imbued with a feeling of naturalness. There is no society that does not both need and seek to maintain its social norms while also allowing for change, whether small or large.

The argument here is that neoliberalism has become the dominant norm that governs us today, and that it functions, as do all social norms, through our internalisation of its values and expectations. This is the ontological change identified by Rose. We have internalised neoliberalism's view of what constitutes a human, what makes a 'successful' human. We have swallowed, and made as if our own, what is required to survive and thrive under the harsh competitive world of neoliberal economics, and we accept as self-evidently true that our survival, or our failures, are matters of our own choice. Thus while neoliberalism is first and foremost a doctrine of political economy, it is also a principle of civilisation that, through a socialisation process, shapes our makeup and frames the meaning of our everyday reality.[13] It fits alongside a hidden story of western culture, the generation within each of us of what has been called the 'divided brain'. Here the abstract, instrumentalist left side of the brain has colonised the contextual, holistic, systemic and humane right brain, leading to a particular and highly limited way of thinking about and conceiving of ourselves and the world.[14] It is thus a wildly imbalanced brain producing a wildly imbalanced worldview.

Most of us do not engage with neoliberalism as a grand strategy, but rather we meet it with its mundane vocabularies and practices, particularly in workplaces, where our conduct is shaped in accordance with performance reviews and evaluations and a new understanding of professionalism based on metrics of inputs and outputs.[15] We can notice, however, that similar themes emerge again and again across many realms of human endeavour. They are exemplified and endlessly regurgitated back to us in celebrity culture,[16] coded into us through the digital world,[17] and find their way even into how yoga clothes are sold to us.[18] That there is resistance, and places of refusal of neoliberalism, does not deny its overarching dominance.

To gather up the many aspects of the psychic structure of the neoliberal subject I suggest an acronym, CARRPP, derived from six ideal 'markers' of the new subject. CARRPP is the ideal and CARRPP is present in all of us to different degrees. Wherever we are located and whatever our circumstances, our task is to make ourselves over according to these six markers. Each of us is required to do the work individually on our selves and to be the resource that we work on. In accordance with this acronym, we can say that the neoliberal subject is Competitive, Autonomous, Resilient, Responsibilised, Perfectible and Positive. Put together, they render us as human capital.[19]

They set the overarching social norm for us of maximising profits for the self, while at the same time being the capital for that self. Managing this tension keeps us busy and anxious and asks of us what is, ultimately, impossible.

Before moving on to explore CARRPP, some additional comments might help. Firstly, while I argue that none of us is immune from neoliberalism, its disciplining power is differential in its impact. Its freewheeling, unfettered self, mobile and independent, is particularly attractive to the young.[20] Class differences too will be played out, given that the neoliberal subject needs resources aplenty. More, the self-surveillance and self-monitoring it requires is directed especially at women. Notions of 'femininity' today are very tightly scripted and every woman now must bear responsibility for her looks, her body shape and her 'life biography', no matter how severe the constraints upon her.[21] Some forms of feminism too have been repurposed as neoliberal cheerleaders, displacing feminism's traditional, collectivist concerns. Thus, neoliberal governmentality does not produce singular identities.

Secondly, I do not argue that the individual markers of neoliberal subjectivity as named in CARRPP are somehow themselves contrary to human flourishing. Many are desirable and valuable. But neoliberalism idealises and sanctifies some aspects of the human condition while wholly repudiating others, producing the divided brain identified earlier. We can think about this in evolutionary terms. We have inherited the egoism and drive that kept us alive while competing with wild animals for shelter and food. But our inheritance also includes altruism and collaboration. Neoliberalism has radically shifted us towards the former.[22] Hence, one of neoliberalism's stealthiest features is that it draws on what seems to be an incontestably natural aspect of human life, but we are disciplined into both believing neoliberalism's claims and manifesting them in our lives as if they are the *all* and the *best* of how we are.

Thirdly, while I offer CARRPP to capture the irreducible conditions of neoliberal subjectivity, it serves as a structural conceit on which to hang the discussion. Each of these conditions bleeds into the other and more could be added, such as flexibility, happiness or resourcefulness. In the everyday, the importance of any one is determined by who is speaking and in what context, be it a psychologist advising on mental health, a politician speaking about education or an economist speaking about national debt. That said, a strong case exists that the first two characteristics, competition and autonomy, are the *sine qua non* of neoliberal subjectivity. Without these, neoliberal subjectivity withers on the vine. If neoliberal ontology is about anything, it is about competition between individual, autonomous beings.[23] CARRPP, thus, serves as a working idea, not an exhaustive typology.

The neoliberal subject is competitive

As stated above, a belief in competitiveness in both economics and ontology is essential for neoliberalism to function. While competitiveness is the very heart of capitalism, and nothing much has changed here, neoliberalism proposes that competition is at the heart of what it means to be human. Paul Mason, economist and television presenter, captures the relationship and the significance succinctly:

> (N)eoliberalism is the doctrine of uncontrolled markets: it says that the best route to prosperity is through individuals pursuing their own self-interest in the market. It says that the state should be small (except for its riot squad and secret police); that uncontrolled financial speculation and inequality are good; that the natural state of humankind is ruthless competition.[24]

I would like to draw out this idea of the self-interested individual some more. Under conditions of neoliberalism, we are reminded constantly that competition is inherently good. It keeps costs down and generates dynamic and efficient growth. Our task is to embrace the belief that human freedom is found in the unleashing of that competitiveness to become that beast known as *homo economicus*. This is the being who is committed to self as a competitive economic unit based on the belief that humans are governed by self-serving interests and behaviour. As neoliberalism believes that the markets are unimprovable, it also believes, as suggested by Hayek decades ago, that all of life can be successfully managed through market forces. In this sense neoliberalism is a form of social Darwinism – a doctrine of the survival of the fittest – and it interprets nature to mean market forces.[25]

Competition between people thus is conceived of as necessary to free up human potential in the same way that competition is conceived of to function in the market-place. In a similar fashion, the individual must be freed from the bonds of others or from dependency on others. Any claims that groups and collective identities might make on us serve to restrain and limit us. They get in the way of our impulse to freedom. Increasingly, the competitiveness of the sports field, in its language and values and its 'science of winning', becomes transferred as a model for human behaviour into politics, business strategy, life coaching and into education.[26] In higher education, for instance, the practice of 'freedom' is shaped by the pressure to excel (over others) and the imperative to do whatever it takes to keep up with one's peers. Education becomes a competition. Students become 'income streams' for institutions that are themselves competing for additional students, for investment and for market share.[27]

In what follows, I explore the negative impact of the competitive value on our psyches. But there is also its social correlative to consider here, the flipside of the competitive norm, found in the argument of neoliberal economics that social welfare is inefficient, counterproductive and patronising. Without the dynamics of competition in, say, housing or healthcare provision, we humans become dependent and lack incentive to improve, with the consequence, the argument goes, that inequality can become solidified. What we get is the 'nanny state', interfering and stultifying. Having to compete for goods, such as homes or medical care, is natural and good, keeps us sharp and active and keeps the market working efficiently. In this view, social bonds constitute a brake on human freedoms.

The neoliberal subject is autonomous

As we saw above, a foundation stone of neoliberalism is the autonomy of the individual, the necessary partner of competitiveness. Here autonomy is understood to refer to a pre-social self, and invulnerable in this to other selves. In this sense, autonomy becomes an ontological condition. We can think about autonomy also as the resource, an enclosed space of human individuality, bounded by the envelope of its skin.[28] This is what constitutes the field of the entrepreneur, the agent who is in control and who acts.

The idea of the autonomous self thus rests on the belief that there is an 'I' that is in control and that is prior to other 'I's. Our duty then is to prioritise the needs and desires of this pre-social 'I'. We must become a 'self-with-distance', literally, our *own* business, inhabiting this entity that exists *before* relationships. We then mediate our relationships with the world and others, via our honed skills and in accordance with business principles.[29] In this way, we can move through the world as individuals, maximising our own interests and needs.

But let's think about this autonomous self a little bit more. Autonomy is folded into and also presupposes a belief about choice. Autonomy says that, given that we are in fact in charge, our destiny is a matter of personal choice and, concomitantly, our responsibility. This autonomous self can choose to be however she wishes: she has the resource (that self) and agency (the very same self) necessary to do so. Hence, we can all be better persons, more efficient, more beautiful, more successful, more attractive. We have the conditions to 'realise' ourselves as if this actually were our own project to be commanded from within. As we saw at the outset, it was this dimension of the newly emerging self that triggered Nikolas Rose's interest: the idea of the 'self' as a project.

According to Barbara Ehrenreich, our belief in autonomy today reproduces a centuries-old theme: our endless absorption with ourselves, but elevated to a new level, to what she calls a deification of the self. Self-help books advise us to love ourselves by, for instance, constructing shrines of ourselves. Behind the books, and other sources of such ideas, is the idea that we are each in control of our physical and emotional bodies. This extends as far as control over ageing, illness and even, increasingly, death. For instance, we are tutored to conceive of our immune system as a resource that we can harness against cancer, say, once we also equip ourselves with the necessary positive attitude. However, recent research suggests that this is not a correct understanding of the immune system. In fact, it has become evident that our bodies are a confederation of parts such as cells and tissues, some of which may seek to advance their own agenda, including the possibility of destroying the whole organism. A person's immune system can act as if it has agency and facilitate the spread of tumours. In other words, microbiology tells us quite conclusively that we are not 'in control'. Our bodies are not resources that we can, with the right effort and skills, control for our own ends.[30]

Coming at the idea of autonomy from a different register, we can think about how notions of autonomy lead also to an instrumental and purposive way of relating to the wider world. We have learned to approach professional and social gatherings as opportunities to network, meaning that we relate to others there through their potential for our individual advancement. More generally, in neoliberal times many relationships are modelled on the idea of a 'contract' in the same way that trade and business function on contract. Parties agree on what is best for them individually and enter into a contract to this effect. Love, parenting, friendships, education can all be governed in this way, if not on paper, then metaphorically. Drawing again on a world I know well – university teaching – I have experienced directly the logic of this idea. Students in third-level institutions are now considered consumers of a product that they have paid for in advance. Teaching staff provide the 'content', set out in learning outcomes for each course. External mechanisms have been devised to monitor if this contract has been met. Meeting the contract, with evidence, becomes a 'key performance indicator' for measuring staff performance. And so it becomes a cycle more concerned with contracted outcomes and their achievement than with an educational process. In another realm entirely, speed dating – a phenomenon of the neoliberal age – we also see a loose assemblage of this idea. Two people contract to a brief meeting in which they quickly assess the potential of the other to meet their needs. Speed dating is purposive: no time is wasted. It is goal-orientated, contained, and follows a set order. Similarly, child-rearing practices and the choice of schools have come to be framed as an investment in a child's future, as a way of maximising their possibilities.

This world of choice and contracts opens up some profound challenges. Choice as an absolute good can swiftly become tyrannical, as is evident when we have to choose toothpaste in the supermarket or, more acutely, when we expect young people to 'choose' their career paths while still in school. What if we make the wrong decision? Outcomes cannot be guaranteed and yet we are asked to choose as if they were and as if we were in charge. The utter contingency of choice makes it terrifying and we have all felt the paralysis that can result. Then there is the implication that, if it is all up to us, we have only ourselves to blame if it all goes wrong.[31] Moreover, too much choice can be deleterious to well-being. Seeking to make rational choices but with limited time and resources produces not a feeling of freedom, but of anxiety.[32] Making the right choice requires us to be in a fairly constant state of comparing ourselves with others and with their choices and outcomes. This creates insecurity and a state of being that is both unhealthy and contrary to what is necessary for human happiness.[33]

The neoliberal self is resilient

Talk of resilience is everywhere today. Its hegemony as a concept reflects perhaps most clearly the disciplining aspect of neoliberalism in the face of economic and political uncertainty.[34] We don't have to look too carefully to find its overt expression or its tone. It is wrapped into workplace management speak, childcare discourses, debates about mental health and young people's employment prospects. We must all become more resilient!

At face value, resilience is a wholly desirable quality. Originally a term coined to refer to the capacity of materials to recover their shape or strength following compression, it is usually used today to refer to a human capacity to experience some kind of rupture but to recover, in fact to bounce back, ideally strengthened by the experience. However, this idea too has taken on ideological status. It now represents a quality we must each individually nurture and 'store'. It becomes obligatory. And if we lack it, we are on our own.

So what does it mean exactly in the context of neoliberalism? To be resilient is to be adaptable, flexible, accepting of the inevitability of hardship and of a difficult landscape 'out there' in a way that allows us to recover and flourish, over and over if necessary. Resilience is framed thus, with tones of emotional sturdiness and a strong inner belief, reflected in a capacity to resist or at least overcome, reasonably swiftly, vulnerability. No matter what we encounter, we can (and ought to) re-enter the fray, stronger, wiser, more resilient still. Resilience is like capital: it generates more of itself. If we are resilient, we can face any adversity as a welcome challenge. In a crisis, we become resourceful and we refuse to surrender. Resilience says that there are no problems, only opportunities. In its functioning as an ideology in neoliberal times, resilience has become a doctrine that 'authenticates who we are as people'.[35]

In this way, the psychic structure of the neoliberal subject is built on an acceptance that insecurity makes us stronger. It allows us to test ourselves, to improve and thrive, and both danger and risk become necessary for the prosperity of life. Resilience becomes our own self-administered and self-developed inoculation against failure. We train ourselves, we work on our emotions and characteristics to ensure that we are able to change, innovate and adapt.

Resilience thus is bound up with our commitment to continuous self-improvement founded on the idea that we are autonomous and in control. We make the commitment to improve our physical and cognitive health through tools and strategies such as mindfulness, wellness and optimum nutrition, but also through health checks and by paying close attention to our hearts, digestive systems, feet and spines. We search for excellence in all aspects of ourselves, we try to weed out or compensate for any 'defects' through multiple 'interventions'. Perversely, however, the more we pursue such meticulous self-management (monitoring our choices, weighing and measuring ourselves and micro-managing the food we eat), the more likely we are to become anxious, narcissistic and guilty, especially when we have slip-ups, get it wrong or make foolish choices.[36]

A critical site for the psychopolitics of resilience is the labour market, where the rule now is that professional success makes a successful person. Employees, and indeed the unemployed, are required to be resilient enterprises selling a service, seeking out clients, managing their own costs, undertaking research, development and training. Throughout this professional competence-building process, both burden and cost are transferred onto the individual, wherein the idea of self-control is cast as compensation for an external world that is impossible to control.[37]

While resilience may indeed work to make us risk-bearing subjects in a precarious world, it also produces a particular kind of disempowerment. Neoliberalism has brought economic insecurity, environmental threats and terrorism, and though ideas of resilience may provide succour, their summative impact diminishes our sense of agency by reducing our cognitive and psychic life to a domain of insecurity.[38] A term often used to describe this world is 'precarity', referring to a state of casual, contingent employment (think: zero hours contracts) that is increasingly the case for the young today but that spills over into a generalised feeling of insecurity. We learn to accept, ironically, that we cannot change the world but must adapt to its threats and dangers. One critical defence against such precarity is a compulsory work ethic and a hyper-entrepreneurialism.

One small example of this process is contained in the best-selling book by Irish author Emilie Pine. Urged on by her university to take on more work, she found herself close to mental and physical collapse. She followed advice and attended a course on mindfulness offered for university staff. There she and her colleagues began to see that, although their stress was created by unrealistic work levels, the course suggested that they ought to be able to 'fix' themselves to be more resilient and carry that stress. In reality they were, she concluded, cannibalising themselves.[39]

Thus, resilience too is a double-edged sword. Who could, reasonably, not wish to be resilient? And yet, in incorporating resilience as wedded to our sense of self, we play for ourselves a card of more, not less, insecurity and embellish and normalise ever further the myth of autonomy.

The neoliberal self is responsibilised

That taking responsibility for ourselves and for the consequences of our actions is a good thing is not at issue here. What neoliberalism has heralded is a specific process called responsibilisation, whereby we are made ontologically responsible for tasks that might previously have been carried out by the state or its agents or by collectivities of people. As the welfare state shrinks, we must take up the slack. Responsibilisation then refers to a political, economic and social process of shifting burdens, once carried socially, back onto individuals. It empties out the social.

However, the neoliberal self needs training in responsibilisation for her own fortunes and choices and, necessarily, her own failures, including the failure to choose to be resilient and responsibilised. Responsibilisation is the necessary close companion of the concept of autonomy. Put very simply, responsibilisation as a 'good' delivers the message that failure is one's own choice/fault. The neoliberal subject must internalise this logic.

How does this work? Presupposing autonomy as ontologically true, it follows that we are in charge of ourselves, and that we manifest this authority over ourselves through the choices we make. If we are in charge of our very own self, then we can choose to be however we wish. As we are urged to become more productive, efficient, self-reliant selves, responsibilisation is naturalised and turns inside out the historic contract of democracy: that we are citizens bound to other citizens in a collective endeavour. Neoliberalism repudiates the social contract and its logic of collective ethics or collective responsibility for the collective, as a drag on economic growth.[40]

Responsibilisation shows up in many subtle ways. We are 'invited' to health checks, audits and screenings whose injunctions and admonitions we feel we cannot resist, for to do so seems to be putting ourselves at great risk. The establishment of new medical norms, such as screening against all manner of possible disease, creates an unease (what if I don't take this possibility?) and at the same time affirms our health as our own responsibility. Of no less importance here is the relationship in the medical world between neoliberal subjectivity and neoliberal capitalism as manifest in private medical care.[41]

This logic gets played out in different ways in our sense of shared endeavour. In times of austerity, responsibilisation can facilitate 'sacrificial citizenship' when those who have not invested in themselves properly as human capital (by hiring life coaches or personal gym instructors or by professional retraining) can be cast aside, deemed impediments to others' freedom or growth. Their sacrifice is justifiable because they did not adequately learn the lesson of independence.[42] As a social norm, therefore, responsibilisation inculcates us to accept that those who don't comply with the rules necessarily suffer the punishment.

These ideas have shaped our attitudes to unemployment, where job seeking has become a job in itself. Working for free, called an 'internship', has become normalised in Ireland. Those seeking work are encouraged to look inward and eradicate internal obstacles, to be positive, energetic, forward-looking and flexible. However, this self-work, or 'life hacking', never ends. We need to mitigate the possibility that our knowledge and skills will become obsolete, we need to keep ourselves competitive. Though presented as a choice, this self-work is, in fact, compulsory and has the quality of entrapment. Having a 'brand', a portfolio of talents and upgraded skills, is required to compete for jobs,[43] and lack of success in the labour market becomes personal failure, or a failure of personhood. Those who make it are rewarded with a guilt-free psyche. They may now enjoy their privileges more, in view of the misery of those who did not make the 'right investment' in themselves.[44] Professional success proves success of personhood.

In the summer of 2017, while beginning this book, I encountered two media stories that perfectly captured the idea of responsibilisation. A full-colour spread in a weekend supplement of an Irish newspaper featured smiling, happy, good-looking people in their fifties and sixties who had all become successful entrepreneurs late in life.[45] Its surface message was unambiguous: older people too can turn their fantasies and hobbies into profitable ventures. All it takes is willpower and the correct upbeat attitude. Under the surface was a darker message, though transmitted with bright cheer: that even those with a labouring life behind them may have to fight for a place in the gig economy of the self-employed, because in a future world, where pensions may not be guaranteed, our fate will be in our own hands. See, the feature said, everyone can rescue themselves through entrepreneurship!

The second story, heard on afternoon radio, was a young woman's account of how she and her partner had been refused a mortgage because of a period she spent receiving treatment for mental health difficulties after a personal trauma. Unable to confirm to the lender that she would not ever be 'at risk' again, she and her partner lost their mortgage approval and their intended home. Her initial, very human response to a difficulty, and her honest appraisal of herself in the face of an impossible demand, rendered her, in the eyes of the insurance industry, an overly risky human. She was found to be an unresponsibilised subject, and paid a severe price.

Both stories, in different ways, delivered a message about responsibilisation. Resilience, entrepreneurial flair and emotional sturdiness are required, and their absence will deliver a cost. Taken together, the stories mark out the polarities of the ideal, successful, entrepreneur and the unacceptably vulnerable human. I stress *unacceptably* vulnerable because, as we will see in the next chapter, neoliberalism has embraced the emotional life of its subjects with gusto but only on condition that it is conducted in very particular ways, i.e. without creating risk. The stories set out crucial aspects of neoliberal subjectivity and reveal its generative practices. Their relaying in the media governs us in the same way that fables and fairy tales help shape children's sense of right and wrong. They lay out what is acceptable and what is not acceptable conduct.

The neoliberal self is perfectible

Of all the ontological conditions of the neoliberal subject, it is perhaps the idea of the perfectibility of the individual that has most saturated popular culture and is nowhere more acutely played out than in the beauty and fashion industries, especially those targeted at younger women, and increasingly, girls. Without any irony, advertising tells us ceaselessly that we can have 'flawless' skin, hair, teeth, limbs and overall looks. The notion of perfectibility that circulates in these multi-billion-euro industries resonates widely in our culture through the paradigm of the makeover. Each of us has the option of being made over, not just through cosmetic surgery and beauty treatments, but through all manner of technologies of the self, from cognitive behavioural therapy (CBT)[46] and fitness regimes to a complete change of wardrobe and a rebranding of our self online.

Beauty apps, now easily available, will determine if you are 'pretty' or 'ugly', and others promise that you can 'swipe your way to beautification'. They constitute a new world of intense and banal surveillance of women's bodies. Their message has deep roots in ideas about personal responsibility and moral accountability for one's body and in entrepreneurial modes of selfhood. With the correct labouring and the willingness to continuously appraise and transform, one can work on blocked pores, veins, moles, wrinkles, eyebrows, skin texture and hair. Such intense self-scrutiny is, of course, always presented as a choice, as fun, as freedom.[47]

Hence the neoliberal subject is kept busy. She is simultaneously a product, a walking advertisement, a manager of her résumé, a biographer of her rationales and an entrepreneur of her possibilities. She is a project that requires upgrading and rebranding in a continuous, self-reliant and self-managed process towards a state of perfection. With tracking and monitoring devices, we can now measure ourselves against idealised humans, monitor our steps, our calorie intake, our biometric markers, count breaths to become more calm and target the right kind of fun. Perfectibility of the self is only an app away.[48]

'Perfectibility' is a concept based on notions of human capacities, suggesting certain conduct that contributes to neoliberalism's governing of the soul. A fascinating meta-analysis of US college students over almost three decades concluded that perfectionism had increased as a response to competitive individualism, evident in three distinct dimensions. Perfectionist beliefs were identified as, first, directed by the students towards themselves, second, towards others, and third, as coming, equally, *from* others. In other words, these students had unrealistic expectations of themselves, were punitive in their self-evaluations, and imposed unrealistic standards and harshly evaluated others around them. Though they believed that their social contexts were excessively demanding, they felt obliged to display perfection in order to secure approval and to mitigate harsh judgement from others.[49] The authors of the report concluded that the heavier burden of market-based competition, and the move away from social equity towards *laissez faire* governance, is overly borne by younger people, who are then obliged to strive against one another for work and for careers.

A cultural norm, identified in the research cited above, is the belief in meritocracy, that the perfect life is available once you try hard enough. Along with its corollary – that failure to achieve the perfect life is a reflection of personal inadequacy – it falsely and insidiously connects such achievement, and indeed wealth itself, with innate personal value. Because in educational systems and in workplaces individuals are, in fact, sifted and sorted into hierarchies, neoliberal meritocracy places a strong need to perform, strive and achieve at the centre of contemporary life.[50] Hence unrealistic expectations abound and young people increasingly define themselves in strict terms of personal achievement, in turn informed by a hyper-individualistic belief in perfectibility.

The neoliberal self is positive

A phenomenon of neoliberalism, as we have seen, is the growth of not only new ideas about human happiness but also 'hucksters' of that happiness,[51] those first identified by Nikolas Rose in the 1980s, who tell us how to achieve happiness: life coaches, psychologists and life-experts of all kinds. The idea is attractively simple: happiness is an achievable and natural state for all humans and is always within reach once we adopt the right, positive attitude towards life and towards ourselves. Who would dare take a critical stance against human happiness and being positive? But we need to think about these ideas as social norms and, given its powerful position, about the role of positive psychology.

Much has been written about the growth of positive psychology as a clinical practice, but also its spillover into everyday talk and understanding.[52] Positive psychology can be understood as a loose amalgam of psychological approaches that makes the case that the potential for happiness is something we all possess and that it can be objectified, mapped, measured and manipulated.[53] Over time, positive psychology has grown to become a powerful presence in our cultures, along with other individualist doctrines of self-mastery such as CBT. [54]At the core of positive psychology is the idea that happiness is a personal choice, a view, it is said, that is supported by the science emerging from research into the brain. If in the past we didn't really know what made people happy, science now claims to know. Neuroscience, specifically, provides us with the correlates of happiness, and its findings are fed into the development of policies for schools and workplaces to bring about the desired behaviour change. Phone apps are available to allow us to track and somehow 'understand' our moods. There is now the potential for all of us to be pushed towards a single view of human optimisation, a script for how we can all be more positive, more happy, more of the time.[55]

Barbara Ehrenreich, quoted earlier in relation to immunology, has written about her experience of the world of positive psychology following a breast cancer diagnosis. She took up the recommendation to go on-line to meet other sufferers but found that her natural inclination to be very real about her experiences was not welcome. Her impulse to honesty was silenced by the demand to be positive. She was told that she should embrace her cancer as an opportunity for spiritual enlightenment and to inspire others. She was encouraged to purchase and utilise pink things such as clothes, diaries and stationery. She was told how to speak about her illness. Putting aside this bruising encounter, she followed up on the science and reached a surprising conclusion: that the data disproves causality between being 'positive' and better treatment outcomes. She began to understand positive psychology as primarily a multi-billion-dollar enterprise.[56]

Ehrenreich's book is a forensic account of positive psychology's functioning as a forceful social norm. Behind the valorisation of positivity, she encountered the converse idea that those who are unhappy are somehow defective. They are unhappy *because* they do not have the right positive attitude. Positive psychology can end up blaming – and/or medicating – individuals for their own misery while refusing to consider the context that might have made them thus.[57] Rather than looking at the effect of social, political and economic institutions and strategies, positive psychology asks us to take responsibility for our own neural or behavioural errors.[58]

Stress expert Russ Harris explains the pervasive myths about happiness as a four-sided trap. First, we are not, in fact, in control of our feelings and thoughts. Second, it is neither desirable nor possible to rid our-selves of negative thoughts and feelings. Third, mental suffering is not an abnormality but a part of life. Fourth, 'happiness' is not the natural state for all humans, as statistics on depression, loneliness and indeed men-tal disorders would suggest. The grand myths of posi-tivity are the source of much unhappiness, keeping us trapped, repeatedly attempting and failing to become happy.[59]

Any consideration of positive psychology inevitably leads us to the current concept of wellness, a concept that was unknown to us until recently but works hard now in our culture. Wellness involves, fundamentally, an injunction to take control of our mental and physical health. We do this through privileging something called 'self-care', through fitness and positive-thinking programmes, diets and exercise, and the work towards wellness is endless. It requires us to, somehow, future-proof ourselves today. Dieting now requires more than counting calories and getting exercise, it also demands diet coaches, attending meetings, keeping a journal, reading diet books and websites, recording data on computer programmes, and sharing our story. What is involved is nothing less than instrumental regulation of the self.[60] Moreover, the rhetoric of wellness is highly moralised: being happy and healthy pass for a moral life. Morality is no longer about the public sphere or an issue of public deliberation, but our lifestyle choices. And as with the happiness phenomenon, the more we try to achieve wellness, the more narcissistic, anxious and isolated we become as we are confronted with the emptiness of our own desires.[61]

We can understand, then, the concepts of self-care and wellness, key dimensions of positive psychology, as a precarious defence. We try for weight loss, for instance, through diet and exercise without questioning the hegemony of fast food, thus eclipsing the role of mass-food production and the intensification of agriculture in our suffering. Moreover, self-care is primarily about a marketable, entrepreneurial self over and above any concept of the relational self, and in suggesting it as the solution to precarity, the idea of the entrepreneurial self is shored up again. Social problems are met with individual solutions. We are schooled to accept that strong affective states, such as loneliness or anxiety, are a failure of our own psychology rather than a sign of the tearing of the social fabric.[62]

We can think about positive psychology's link to neo-liberalism then across two dimensions. Firstly, positive psychology ends up banishing what is considered negative. It says that we must manifest and strive towards happiness through the eradication of negative thoughts or emotions. It says that we are responsible for our own happiness. Through the valorisation of positivity, neoliberalism reifies our biological lives as the domain of agency and self-governance.[63] Secondly, this notion fits snugly with neoliberalism's repudiation of the social. As the burden of mental and other suffering is shifted onto the sufferers themselves, mental health becomes a form of personal mental hygiene to assist people to accept this new reality. Both economic and psychic pain are framed as coming from the same sources: a lack of efficiency and productivity, an inability to accept reality and to be positive. The treatment corrects and realigns how we individually reason and think. An expectation of support from the state signifies an error of judgement, though one that can be corrected.[64]

Conclusion

As might have become evident, it is difficult to cleanly distinguish between the different dimensions of neoliberal subjectivity presented through the acronym CARRPP. Each dimension is woven into the other in a sturdily self-perpetuating, reinforcing fabric and its values are quietly smuggled into our lives without much fuss. Together, these dimensions suggest an ideal type, but all dimensions are played out in many different aspects of our lives. If we pay close attention, we will notice the ubiquity of discourses of autonomy, resilience, self-care, positivity, of changing the 'narratives' in our heads and of learning to see everything as a growth opportunity. Of course, there is nothing intrinsically wrong with any of these as dimensions of the human experience. What I have tried to present here, drawing on what is just a slice of the scholarly work in this area, is twofold. First is that, under neoliberalism, these dimensions have taken on an ideological quality, and second is that they all silence the social in our selves. In its stead they deliver the competitive, autonomous individual, in control, responsibilised and resilient, who accepts that there will be losers and winners and, while this might generate some discomfort, understands that the losers are those who made the wrong choices. The social is banished from our sense of self, ethics is replaced with function and responsibility applies only for the self.

Thus, the neoliberal subject has become a degraded subject at the very level of her being, stripped of what is necessary for her flourishing and growth. She has become ontologically atomised. In the chapters to follow, I treat two particularly powerful modes of ontological socialisation that have taken off in the era of neoliberalism: therapy culture, and the mindfulness movement. Both very specifically offer a version of what it means to be a human. The latter, as we will see, is of particular interest because of its roots in Buddhist thought.

The Self as Anxious Monad Caught in Therapy Culture

A t first glance it might seem that the neoliberal era cares deeply about our emotional and psychological worlds. As we saw, the neoliberal self pays close attention to what goes on in her head. Workplaces have anti-bullying strategies, primary schools have mental health committees with pupil participation, newspapers, radio and social media are replete with stories of personal triumph over depression, alcoholism, grief and self-harm. Hardly a day goes by without some expert – be it a life coach, psychologist or trainer – offering us guidance on how best to live our lives, how to be happier, more fulfilled and have better relationships. It is as if all of our insecurities, anxieties, low moods and disturbances are taken seriously but also that many creative solutions are easily available to us to reduce our suffering. Surely, it could be argued, this is an unmitigated good thing, especially as we seem to be in the midst of unprecedented levels of mental ill health?

When I first conceived the idea for this book, I had few thoughts about this daily phenomenon other than acknowledging its existence, but over time, as I listened carefully, I began to think that something else was going on. It became clear to me that, while we now certainly talk more about and seem to have a better understanding of our emotional lives, and while such openness to emotional honesty is surely welcome, there is also a way in which, while seeming to offer us liberation, some of the ways that we talk and think seem to deepen our suffering. This chapter addresses this apparent contradiction by arguing that it illustrates perhaps the most disturbing aspect of neoliberal governance: the way we have internalised its cruelties as our salvation. One of the means of internalisation is through what is termed the 'therapy culture', a recent phenomenon that is characterised by a very particular mindset.

The argument I make in this chapter is in two parts. Firstly, I accept and build on the view that a significant cause of our current distress, manifest in increased incidences of anxiety and depression, is neoliberalism itself, specifically in its view of what it means to be human: the kind of person captured in the previous chapter. This is, in the words of an Irish psychotherapist, the 'anxious monad' – the term 'monad' borrowed from mathematics, where it signifies a single, isolated unit.[65] Secondly, I explore the role of therapy culture as co-causal in this suffering through its ceaseless circulation of ideas about self-regulation, resilience, happiness and autonomy. As we painfully manifest the disorders of neo-liberalism, we lean on the tools and strategies provided in therapy culture, which, in identifying the 'problem' as being within our own heads exclusively, occludes the role of neoliberalism in our misery and leaves us feeling worse.

While therapy culture may find echoes in therapy rooms, and they are not entirely discrete phenomena, the idea refers to something that has power outside the traditional, confined and relational spaces of psycho-therapy[66] and my critique here concerns therapy culture only. Thus, I wish to make clear that this book has no quarrel at all with the good and often life-saving 'psy' professions, some practitioners of which, as cited throughout these pages, share this critique. I also wish to make clear that I do not suggest that all mental suffering is caused by late-capitalism. I accept the biopsycho-social model for our state of minds: that biology, psychology and social factors always feature.[67] There is, however, a constant, direct relationship between forms of social organisation and mental disorder, and diagnostics in relation to human behaviour are themselves subject to norms that change. It should be no surprise that our diagnostics and cures are shaped by neoliberal thinking.

This chapter will not just touch on debates about the politics of diagnostics but will follow, instead, what happens if we consider mental disorders as signs of social distress, or of sickness in the social order, albeit borne heavily by those individuals involved.[68] What if today's disorders were a manifestation of neoliberalism's penetration of our psyches? In what follows I draw on writers who make this case and then move on to the role of therapy culture.

Neoliberalism: the age of anxiety

We are today – in Ireland and elsewhere – exercised by the state of our mental health. It is not unusual to hear talk of an epidemic, and there is a popular view that things are getting worse for us.[69]

Indeed, the evidence seems to support such an argument. According to World Health Organization data in 2017, slightly more than one in ten people globally live with a mental disorder, the largest number recorded. Diagnosed anxiety has increased in Ireland, and the rate of people taking antidepressants rose by 28 per cent between 2012 and 2017.[70] Millennials feature prominently in the troubling statistics. Despite the greater investment in health and wellness, compared to previous generations, among that cohort, major depression tops the list of both mental and physical disorders.[71] Young people are five times more likely to be mentally ill today compared with sixty to seventy years ago.[72]

A recent training I attended in my own university was illustrative. We heard that social phobia had become the most common condition encountered by the counselling service. That is, students were struggling with the tasks of being with other people, making eye contact and talking to strangers. The simple expectation of beginning conversations had become difficult. Their experience, we were told, did not arise from the quotidian social anxiety we all feel in situations where some degree of performance is required or when we are in the company of strangers, but indicated something quite severe that was having a negative impact on their attendance and functioning. The *Growing Up in Ireland* research, which tracks health data for young people, reported in November 2019 that one quarter of twenty-year-olds surveyed had experienced relatively high levels of stress and depressive symptoms. The number of Irish adolescents experiencing 'very severe anxiety' had doubled from 2012 to 15 per cent.[73] And even younger people are of concern, as indicated by a proposal from the Irish Association for Counselling and Psychotherapy (IACP) that counselling be made available in primary schools. Loneliness and isolation have become a factor for many people in Ireland, reflected in a reported increase in the number of callers to the Irish Samaritans in 2019.[74]

So how do we explain these trends? Are they a function of some biological (or biochemical) disruption? Or childhood conditioning? Or, in the case of students, are they a function of the pressurised environment of third-level education? Or perhaps the explanation is simply that those students were now willing to seek help when, at another time, they would suffer silently? Answering these questions immediately brings us into the tricky arena of proving causality in complex sets of relationships. As stated earlier, the relationship between social mores and what is considered dysfunctional behaviour certainly shapes how and what we diagnose. In Victorian times, women were diagnosed with psychological conditions that are no longer considered valid, replaced in salience today by diagnoses of depression and anxiety.[75] Take 'opposition defiant disorder', now recognised as a mental disorder in children but unknown up to recently. Was it, therefore, 'discovered' as a disorder that had simply never been acknowledged as such, though always present? Or was it brought forth, 'created' as a disorder by the availability of a label. Is there any relationship between its acceptance as a medical condition now and the impact of the stress of contemporary family life on children? Two other medicalised conditions, general anxiety disorder (GAD) and social phobia, the latter referred to above, have relatively recently entered into our diagnostic tool kit. Shyness too, once considered a normal human trait, is now diagnosed as an unhealthy state of mind, a component of social phobia.

The debates about whether disorders or certain behaviours and attitudes are mental illnesses (the medical model) or emotional/psychological manifestations of social distress (the psychosocial model) are not just significant for the 'cure' in terms of the individual sufferer but also for what they reveal about our social order. As we saw in the previous chapter, neoliberalism has created new social norms around human conduct. Being 'normal' today means fully committing ourselves to competition, autonomy, responsibilisation, and so on. But it doesn't take long before those who don't or won't make these commitments – such as, for instance, people who are depressed or anxious – are considered dysfunctional, or disturbed in some way, and are pathologised.[76] What this means, socially, is that we are off the hook from having to think collectively about what is actually making us anxious and depressed. Moreover, once we explain our distress through 'illness', and not social causes, we then necessarily accept that the cure is individualised. If the 'cure' fails, then it is tough luck: we must suffer on alone.

Barbara Dowds, a geneticist and psychotherapist, rejects the idea that the current patterns relating to depression and anxiety are explicable by genetics or biology. For her, the psychosocial realm offers us explanations.[77] In the same vein, Belgian psychoanalyst Paul Verhaeghe argues that the rates of and nature of mental affliction are not coeval with but are, in fact, caused by the impact of the deeper penetration of market-based values into our social order. Our struggles now, such as acute doubts about our identity and about the purpose or meaning of life, cannot be interpreted as a continuation of age-old existential questioning. They have become disorders produced by the nature and rate of social change.[78]

The case for neoliberalism as a cause of our mental distress and suffering takes many different forms. Below I capture some of these arguments and their convergence on the common ground of explaining the psychopolitics of the neoliberal self, drawing attention to the key theme of the evacuation of the social.

Let's recall again the changed role of the state under neoliberalism. As we saw, neoliberalism involves a rolling back of the state. In western liberal democracies, an important function of the state is to uphold the idea of the commons, or the common good. This translates into the provision of public goods such as public transport, socialised medicine, public parks, support for the arts, sport, and so on. It would be naive to deny that the state is immune to capture by sectoral interests and, moreover, the 'common good' can be reduced to competing visions of the good life. Nonetheless, this model of statehood is informed by the idea that there is a social contract between all of us that is not reducible to the sum of all our needs, or about satisfying individual/sectoral needs, but that cherishes the very idea of society itself as inherently valuable for human flourishing. In this vein, we can say that this kind of state provides something akin to the healthy and supportive environment – the container – that, in the best of all worlds, parents provide for their children so that they might grow and flourish.

One psychoanalytic perspective suggests a way of thinking through what happens to us as citizens when the state is in retreat under conditions of neoliberalism. Its impact is similar to the impact on a child of alcoholic or psychologically absent parents who create a poor or disrupted holding environment for that child. Where parents are out of tune with a child's emotional and material needs, she quickly learns that little good can be expected to come her way. She may conclude that she – with her messy needs and vulnerabilities – is the problem. It is her own fault that life is fraught with danger and insecurity. Moreover, given her dependency, it is not safe for her to acknowledge the inadequate parental caregiving. To cope with this terrible dilemma, she cuts herself off from her caregivers and turns inward.[79]

Extending this analysis, what is lost in the shift towards marketisation and privatisation is the holding provided by the welfare state, the safety net for all citizens, the site for the redistribution of goods in accordance with transparent principles such as equality and justice. But lost too is the sense of collective endeavour, of solidarity and of the social in our being. As we experience an external environment without a state to mediate marketplace excesses, to mitigate inequalities and to provide some sense of security, whatever our condition or abilities, we can become closed down and turn inwards, blaming ourselves. If there is no society, or if it is in retreat around us, we can, like poorly supported children, feel marooned, isolated, anxious and alone. The state, now operating according to market values and market-infused notions of efficiency, becomes impervious to our needs; it has become deadened to the life of its citizens.[80] Like the alcoholic parent, the neoliberal state deprives us of the environmental provisions necessary to thrive.

While this perspective may seem abstract, it does reveal something about the retreat of the state and what arises in its wake, and allows us think about the materiality of that retreat as having psychological dimensions for all of us. Let's take the very real retreat of the Irish state from housing provision in the past decade or so. Without any ambiguity, the state turned its face away from the housing needs of its citizens and towards, instead, property investors, developers and the rule of 'market forces'. Over many years, we followed the catastrophic impact of this decision, evidenced painfully in both statistics and human stories. We listened too to justificatory words by politicians when called upon to defend the disaster. Their messages generally followed a pattern. There was an expression of sorrow for the human misery, which was followed swiftly by a reiteration of the state's changed role in housing provision. We cannot interfere in market forces, we were told, it is not the role of government to do so. These messages communicated many things. They affirmed the logic of privileging market forces: that citizens must fight it out over the goods available. They also reminded us more generally that there's little the state will do for us and, when it acts, it will not be guided by principles of justice or to secure basic human need, even when children are involved. And we were being reminded of the other mantra: this is how it is now, old ways of doing things are no longer appropriate, they confined both us and our spirits.[81] It is surely no surprise then that the *Growing Up in Ireland* report, referred to earlier, which revealed high rates of depressive feelings among our twenty-year-olds, featured their concerns about housing and future financial and employment security.[82]

As with the housing crisis in Ireland, the state's retreat under neoliberalism is rationalised by powerful beliefs about the greater and more efficient role of the markets to provide for all human needs. In this world, the concept of society is replaced by notions about the marketplace, where competition and entrepreneurialism are all that matter. Thus, contracts, rules and regulations proliferate, which, without the symbolic authority found in the idea of society, results in the survival of the fittest.[83] Life becomes, in the words of two other authors in this *Síreacht* series of books, a race to stay in the race.[84] The Ken Loach film *Sorry We Missed You* captures one family's struggle to stay afloat in the sea of neoliberal practices: zero-hours contracts, bogus 'self-employment', with all costs borne by family members, frantically trying to survive.

As the psychoanalytical analysis presented above illustrates, neoliberalism brings with it feelings of abandonment (you are on your own) but also feelings of being impinged upon (high levels of performance expected). Together, they undermine the kind of supportive environment we need to thrive, producing instead stress and feelings of loss. To survive well, we are required to become powered up with norms that are now socially validated: individualism, entitlement and a competitive aggression. We are urged to accept that our freedom is infinite and restricted only by our own minds. But the lack of a container, in fact, is inimical to the human need for boundaries.[85] We find it hard to deal with the expansive, infinite world that we are told is ours. We miss the nourishment of and connection with others required to bring meaning to life, and this absence produces much of our mental suffering.[86] Depression thus can be understood as a collapse of the individual under an over-reaching ego that rejects all authority other than its own will-driven impulse.[87] Here is the breeding ground for the anxious human, who has become a monad: a solitary, single unit. In this way, neo-liberalism's requirement that we accept precarity as normal can produce a psychic collapse in us similar to that which children experience in the face of trauma: a diffuse fearfulness, an anxiety because there is no social body or group skin to brace our fall. We end up blaming ourselves for what is at root a social problem. Thus, our acceptance of precarity as 'how things are' is like a defence against primitive isolation and against becoming a 'nobody', dropped by the social body on which every individual ontologically depends.[88]

In this competitive world, young people in particular are encouraged to instrumentalise themselves. They learn to 'perform a persona' both for the benefit of the ego and for various audiences, and in order to eliminate competition. This task can be summarised by the notion that every person can (and should) have their own 'brand' and/or can 'rebrand' themselves.[89] Most of this activity requires time online. But here too, while keeping people connected in a way never imagined previously, social media's highly visual culture encourages a sense of not being good enough, of dissatisfaction with body image. However, the more time we spend on social media, the greater the chance of anxiety and depression.[90] Measuring others against some notion of perfection, whether it is skin tone and eyelash length or child-rearing practices, we also measure ourselves. Committing ourselves to judging others on social media, for instance, we turn the same scrupulosity back on ourselves, and inevitably come up short. In this context, the social phobia experienced by students in my own university – and the third most frequent psychiatric disorder in the West after alcoholism and depression – may be understood to arise in the culture of judgement and surveillance, a manifestation of cultural and social norms rather than a medical illness.[91]

A common manifestation of neoliberal values in workplaces is the performance review, a powerful tool for shaping our subjectivity. It rests on a belief that our success depends, above all, on *individual* effort and talent. In turn, these are measured by prescribed indicators (how much of anything produced, how many satisfaction rates, and so on) but also by characteristics considered necessary, such as being result-orientated or having the capacity to sell ourselves and talk ourselves up. Performance indicators, then, are utilised subtly, and sometimes not so subtly, to legitimise subsequent pressure on employees to achieve more and more, and the process often draws on soft language such as 'stretching' and 'leaning in'. Other characteristics can get thrown into the mix of indicators, such as 'flexibility' and traits such as 'cheerfulness'. A subsequent failure to perform this new persona brings consequences for our pay, promotion or the terms of our contract. Hence, performance reviews have come to mean more than assessing our work; they creep into the realm of normalising how we ought to be as persons. They sometimes require us to be other than how we are. Inevitably, they create anxiety, and that anxiety can create further emotional turmoil ('I shouldn't be feeling stressed') that is internalised by the individual as her own fault: a state of being that can produce depression.[92]

Performance reviews are merely one aspect of neoliberal workplaces. There is also nonstop change (restructuring, new software, mergers, external assessments), more and more administration and bureaucracy (forms for everything, including forms to manage other forms), and dispiriting contradictions, such as cost-cutting while vast amounts are spent on new systems and consultants' fees.[93] All shape us as workers, producing a hierarchy of winners and losers, the latter powerless to change or revolt for fear of losing out further. Disempowerment is an integral part of how stress, depression and anxiety arise.[94]

The case made here is that the rates of anxiety, depression and social phobia can be understood as caused by changed conditions specific to neoliberalism. Where neoliberalism posits social forms as stultifying and privileges instead the autonomous individual, we can see the negative impact on that individual of the stripping of the social. Where neoliberalism advocates the cultivation of resilience and positivity to survive the new economic reality, we can see instead the impact of the loss of community belonging, social holding and security. Not only have we an economic model that mitigates precisely the psychological attributes (resilience, self-mastery) it depends on, but its social norms in relation to emotional or psychological distress – that we must each carry the cost and bear the risk of such distress – further destroy the ties that create the idea of society while drilling us for maximum performance in the economy.[95]

In the next section, I turn my attention to the role of therapy culture in this process, focusing in particular on its attendant evacuation of the social from our sense of self.

Therapy culture and the trick of neoliberalism

Our exploration of therapy culture's role in emptying out the social from what it means to be human begins with a brief reminder. What I am addressing here is a very contemporary condition, a psychological mindset that is characterised by a cultural obsession with 'curing' or 'fixing' ourselves. The cure and the fix, as we will see, accord with a very narrow script. Whatever we are feeling, be it stress, loneliness or anxiety, the solution, we are told, lies inside our own, separate skulls. Therapy culture functions through all kinds of new professions, norms and practices by normalising values that fit seamlessly with neoliberal inequality and competition,[96] and it turns our critical voices inwards,[97] diverting our attention away from the social and the political. Thus, therapy culture, as understood here, is not just defined by its interpretation of behaviour through the highly individualised idiom of therapeutic discourse, but also because it does so in accordance with a limited vision that recasts social problems as emotional ones.[98] Its beating heart is the in-control individual, the self-willed person, committed to the pursuit of self-improvement and normalised as the correct and good vision of selfhood.[99]

The origins of therapy culture lie, perhaps not surprisingly, in the US, and most particularly in the 1950s, when psychoanalysis began to be of interest to a wider audience.[100] As the psychological disciplines expanded, attempts to standardise human well-being led to the marriage of cultural values of individualised moral responsibility and market freedom, and psychological thinking. More recently many of these ideas gained traction in identity politics, informed too by post-modernity's valorisation of subjectivity and its rejection of the collective. Its ideas were easily soaked up to support psychologically informed suppositions about individual identity, personal responsibility and freedom.[101] There is a complex history of ideas here, but what can be drawn out is the manner in which ideas from within therapy, such as the emphasis on autonomy and self-fulfilment and the elevation of subjectivity, were merged with foundation American myths of individualism and human freedoms and a de-socialised ethic of self-regulation.[102]

While therapy culture is acutely embedded in US culture, it has found a home in many places. A common explanation for its salience in western countries generally is secularisation. It has provided a place we can go to where once we may have participated in religious ritual or practices. I am sure I am not the first person to conceive of much of our daytime radio chat shows as very contemporary, extended confession boxes. However, it can also be said that therapy culture and the therapeutic constitute a new form of religion, rather than symbolising the death of religion. It is no coincidence that therapy culture functions in ways similar to systems of moral prohibition found in religious institutions.[103] For Nikolas Rose, therapy culture's 'high priests' are, as we saw, life coaches, psychologists, spiritual directors, inspirational speakers and other such 'engineers of the soul'.[104]

While a cultural phenomenon, therapy culture calls on and is in synchronicity with other phenomena. One concerns developments in neuroscience, which tells us that the brain is 'plastic', or malleable, and thus human adaptive capacities are great. And one thing we can do to improve our brain, we are told over and over now, is to think 'positively'. Remarkably, the new brain language, talk of its adaptability and flexibility about de-localisation and neural networks, echoes the language of political economy under neoliberalism.[105] We must also consider the impact of trends within the psychological professions. In the UK, during Margaret Thatcher's era, the model of mental treatment that rose to dominance framed the cause of mental illness as belonging at the level of individual orientation or attitude. Hence, individualised solutions, often emphasising cognitive patterning such as learning to think differently, were the answer. The person experiencing distress caused by workplace exploitation was treated thus as a victim of a personal breakdown.[106] Within therapy spaces, mental health treatment has largely moved away from relational approaches towards predominantly individualistic doctrines of self-mastery found in positive psychology and CBT. A recent article by an Irish psychotherapist raised concerns about marketplace values infiltrating the psychotherapy profession here.[107]

That shift has cast a long shadow. Take the case of young writer Hanna Jameson, related in an Irish newspaper, whose early twenties were marked by persistent job, financial and housing insecurity. Hanna sought help for her distress and was diagnosed, in her own words, as bipolar with a 'side order' of borderline personality disorder. She was told that her problems were in her own head and that she would be unwell for the remainder of her life. Her treatment was medication and CBT. However, following a significant improvement in her financial situation and a relationship change, her symptoms eased. The precarity of stagnant wages, insecure housing and increased living costs no longer destabilised her. It was not until years later, however, that she could see this clearly: that her mental anguish had been lifted primarily by financial security. She wondered why her treatment had emphasised her need to recognise 'irrational' thought patterns without recognising the psychological impact of the hopeless circumstances within which she lived.[108]

Therapy culture ideas are easily found, filling radio and television content, in online courses, sold in books and on apps and mainstreamed in workplaces, schools and other places of education and training. We have already considered some of its powerful drivers, the happiness and wellness industries, and a later chapter will explore what has been called the 'McMindfulness' industry. The complex relationship between 'therapy' and 'culture' found in therapy culture is exemplified beautifully in the book *Eat, Pray, Love* by Elizabeth Gilbert, the story of one woman's life transformation through 'self-care', 'spirituality' and the pursuit of pleasure in faraway places through consumption of ice cream and exotic rituals. A well crafted and funny book, its success is also partially explained by its harmonisation with therapy culture values. It is utterly a book of our times. It promises redemption and transcendence via an individual and somewhat eclectic pursuit of personal meaning. And those inspired by it can also buy thematic jewellery, tea and prayer beads online, and visit temples and yoga centres. The world Gilbert conjures up, both retail and spiritual, explicitly targets women seeking emancipation, self-fulfilment and self-betterment.[109]

Indeed, many have noted a new form of feminism that mirrors neoliberalism. It offers a vision for success in business and in the workplace that is tightly bound to a very particular view of what 'feminine' looks and acts like. Success requires pursuing self-interest while conforming to strict routines for beauty, dieting, exercise and hair removal.[110] Women's magazines enjoy a very extensive audience for their not-so-subtle expression of therapy culture. The 'confidence movement' promotes positive thinking by women for just about every aspect of their lives, from workplace relationships to maintaining a 'bikini body', all requiring a particular form of feminine labour that makes women responsible for their looks, success and fortunes.[111]

The amorphousness of therapy culture sometimes keeps it hidden from clear view. One example I encountered recently was a radio interview with the Irish phenomenon of Pippa O'Connor Ormond, known as a 'social influencer', author, former model, fashion designer, seller of clothes, homeware and a certain kind of lifestyle. She is a serial entrepreneur whose energy and resourcefulness exemplify the spirit of neoliberalism. In the interview she explained the role of positive psychology in her success, and one of her messages was that we can all be whomever we wish. Her comments were not exceptional in terms of customary media approaches today to life biographies. But I was struck by one rather throwaway remark. She told the interviewer that when she is not feeling so positive, she doesn't do social media. She doesn't go back online, she said, until 'I am feeling myself again'.[112] I understood this to mean that she could not be 'herself' except when feeling positive.

The re-shaping of subjectivity described here helps explain the way in which therapy culture privatises stress. In workplaces now we are likely to be 'invited' to take responsibility for both increased workload and decreased job security. And we are more likely to respond to work-related stress by attempting to better organise our time, attend mindfulness classes, take medication or try therapy, than to embark on collective action such as through our trade unions. In other words, we have become used to the idea that stress is best addressed through individualised techniques and that we are, in the end, responsible for its production.[113]

Ideas about individual responsibility for emotional or psychological disturbance have become the bedrock of therapy culture. They are seductive, not least because they resonate as highly desirable and seemingly natural. At the risk of being repetitive: who would not want to be successful and happy? But therapy culture serves ideological functions to both discipline us and remind us of the price to be paid for nonconformity. If we do not submit, we can be judged personal failures, lazy or moral hazards. In post-socialist states of Eastern Europe, for instance, ideas of self-help and enterprise became a moral corrective to what was believed to be a defective Soviet-era persona, a person without self-value: a 'loser' in the transition to capitalism.[114] Political transition was linked therefore to the necessity of a wholly new person who, like the client of positive psychology, accepts that she can eradicate unwelcome symptoms and personality flaws.

As the state withdraws from its traditional functions and as social bonds are eroded to create new or more intense forms of insecurity and uncertainty, a need arises to manage this uncertainty. It is in this space that therapy culture has been institutionalised. While the science of subjective feelings is relatively new, its implications have been adopted enthusiastically by policy-makers and by political leaders. Our very human need for hope and joy is drawn into infrastructures of measurement, surveillance and governance. We can now identify the markers of the ideal 'biomedical citizen': adaptable, flexible, self-contained. We can also identify those who fail to shape their brains accordingly or who are at risk of failing. We can, without guilt, blame individuals for their own misery and misfortune and we can ignore the conditions that produced their misery in the first place.[115]

Therapy culture sets out and reaffirms the idea that we are both in control of and responsible for our life chances and our mental health and well-being. We think about distress in idealistic, individualised terms, accepting that, if we change how we think about our difficulties and distresses, we can change our world.[116] The traces of neoliberalism are thus kicked over.

Threaded through this critique is the thematic denial of the social. Rather, therapy culture produces and reaffirms the individualised, solitary person – the monad – as an ontological truth. When we speak therefore of neoliberalism's negative impact on the psyche, it is not that neoliberalism denies human needs, including psycho-social needs, rather it provides us with a way of thinking about these needs and how to meet them, in a manner that further perpetuates the very model self that is the problem. The toll of neoliberalism's heightened individualism and competitiveness is understood through diagnostic categories such as anxiety and depression, with attendant biological or cognitive explanations for which there is treatment, usually individualised therapeutic approaches. In this way, the pathologisation of normal human emotions and behaviour is both a component and a co-constituent of neoliberal subjectivity.[117] The depth of our human experience, our internal emotional world, is now externalised onto the surface of our selves wherein it is named, categorised and treated in accordance with individualised interventions. The story of Hanna Jameson, related earlier, captures key aspects of the critique offered here, wherein our existential and psychological dilemmas are not understood within collective meaning systems but are translated into technical matters about the most effective way of managing malfunction and improving the quality of our life.

Conclusion

The argument made in this chapter is based on two related points. Firstly, the case is made for neoliberalism as significantly causal of the current phenomenon of mental illness, best understood as, in the words of Dowds, a phenomenon of disorders of self. In the second instance, I suggest that therapy culture steps into the frame by promising ameliorative techniques and interventions that in fact produce a self modelled on the requirements of neoliberalism, therefore serving to make us more 'sick'. This model is the 'post-social' subject, the subject stripped of the social.

There is, however, a complex dance being played out here. As someone who grew up in a time when feelings were not spoken of (indeed, as a child I bizarrely assumed that to be an adult meant not having emotions at all), I welcome the new cultural acceptance of our emotions. But I quake at therapy culture's depoliticising of the environmental causes of human suffering and distress through its normalisation of the isolated individual whose freedom is found 'inside her own head'.[118] It has become clear to me that neoliberalism has heralded an unhealthy obsession with the emotions and with therapy-infused discourses.

David Smail argues that any society that creates distress in its members is highly likely to develop institutional systems for distracting attention from the more unfortunate consequences and absorbing their worst effects. In such circumstances, preventing critical analysis from extending beyond the individual to society itself would be advantageous, and rational evidence is likely to be the last thing anyone takes notice of.[119] One powerful way in which neoliberalism occludes its role in our distress is its refusal of the 'collective constitution' of the subject.[120] Yet, as one of the authors cited extensively here, Verhaeghe, points out, therapy culture's individualism, ironically, results in people being more fearful, less trustful of each other and quicker to respond with aggression. Powerlessness and helplessness are toxic emotions. A major cross-cultural comparative research project, much cited in these kinds of discussions, shows that high-income inequality (the bigger the gaps between rich and poor) produces greater mistrust in society and diminishes broader social relationships. Trust is replaced by aggression, fear, less participation in collective life and low health outcomes, especially for the less well-off. More unequal societies are the unhappiest, and inequality breeds depression and anxiety.[121]

We can understand, then, that the daily content of therapy culture, which always turns our gaze inwards, both disciplines and distracts us from the depredations of neoliberalism. Feeling distressed, lonely and isolated, or just plain miserable, we reach for self-help books, listen to inspirational podcasts and trawl the internet alone for help. We will find all kinds of things, but we will also find an endlessly repeated idea that the solution is 'within': located in how we think about the world, in something called our self-esteem, in our self-belief and in our capacity for self-direction. We learn that the cure is some kind of personal rehabilitation, lifestyle tweaks and adaptations, and not, most definitely not, the pursuit of political or social change.[122]

In stripping the 'other' from our sense of self,[123] the therapy culture of the neoliberal world strips us of what it means to be human. The good news is that there is a whole other way of thinking about the relationship between self and other, and this is what is addressed in the next chapter: a Buddhist account of the self.

A Buddhist Account
of the Self

Over ten years ago I attended a thronged public talk in Galway given by a Tibetan monk. Arriving late, I squeezed into the crowd inside the door and it wasn't long before I began to feel very uncomfortable. There was little air in the room and the atmosphere was, somehow, tense, reflecting perhaps the intensity of the topic. The monk himself was kind, playful, and as he took questions from the audience he leaned into us from the stage, smiling encouragingly and openly, his words always simple. But I began to wonder if he was not in some kind of trouble, jet-lagged or dehydrated. His words never changed, regardless of the questions from the floor. If you go looking for your self, he said, no matter how hard you look, you won't find it. You won't locate it. It is not there. You can look and look. But you won't find your self. No matter how hard you try. Smiling all the while, he endlessly repeated a version of these words, over and over.

In fact, he was mirroring the 'stuckness' of the audience. We were the ones in trouble. That is, troubled in accepting his message, given its stark opposition to our Judaeo-Christian inheritance of the idea that each of us possesses, somewhere inside of us, an eternal, essential and unique part that may (or may not) live on after death. For most, religious and non-religious alike, this is our soul. His account too was troublesome for our more secular, everyday ideas about self-esteem and self-reliance. The cornerstone of all such ideas is a strong sense of 'I'.[124] There must be some 'self' to esteem and to rely upon, something that abides eternally, that has a quality of survivability even in the face of very challenging circumstances such as trauma or addiction.

What the monk set out that evening was a classical Buddhist account of the self. It says that the self is irreducibly relational, irreducibly social, constituted by relationships and without permanence or essence. This account precludes the possibility of souls, at least when understood as some entity that is individual, unique and eternal. A Buddhist view of human subjectivity is thus deeply confounding and countercultural to western thought systems and beliefs. It can seem slippery and evasive, difficult even to put into words. As the kindly monk pointed out repeatedly, it is not something to be grasped in our minds but needs to be experienced, and over and over. Try it for yourselves, he told us. Try to go beyond the words and concepts to really experience whether and where and how this 'self' that we seek – the strong sense of an 'I', a permanent, stable self –

exists. His guarantee was that we would simply fail.

In this chapter, I set out a Buddhist account of the self in some detail, thus rising to the challenge that it is difficult to grasp its meaning by words or ideas alone. My intention here, however, is to illustrate a different kind of challenge – to set out a notion of self which provides what I believe is both a true account and a radical alternative to neoliberal subjectivity. In so doing, it also suggests a way of thinking about how it is that neoliberalism has so deeply shaped our subjectivity today and why it is that we are so vulnerable to its colonisation of our minds and psyches. To do this I shall have to treat, necessarily, some different language and different concepts and enter into consideration of Buddhist ontology or a Buddhist account of what it means to be a human. In particular, we need to understand the Buddhist explanation as to how the idea of a permanent, stable self arises so as to seem natural and is taken for granted as an unassailable truth about being human. Thus, I will speak further on in this chapter of something called *skandhas*, or aggregates, whose interplay produces the idea that a self exists, and of two other concepts. One is captured in the Pali term *anatta*, translated into English as 'non-self' or sometimes 'emptiness of self'; the other is the idea of dependent origination, translated thus from the Pali term *pratityasamutpada*. Vietnamese Zen teacher Thich Nhat Hanh, whose many books are widely read in the West, including Ireland, translates this Pali word into the very succinct term 'inter-being', allowing us to make the statement that we 'inter-be' rather than we 'are'.

Anatta, or non-self, is often interpreted outside the Buddhist world as involving some kind of negation of humanity,[125] a view that is, as we will see, wildly incorrect. *Anatta* argues not for nihilism but that there is no permanently abiding, essential entity at the centre of our being. What we call 'self', it says, is empty of permanence. It is constantly changing, constantly in flux. There is nothing eternal here. Over time, we naturalised the idea of self as marked by eternality in order to help us make sense of what it means to be human, and in the West it remains deeply buried in our cultural inheritance from our traditional religious belief systems. But it is a delusion. What exists, rather, is a continuously evolving pattern.[126] We are empty of 'self' but are filled with the outcome, or the process, of our dependent origination. To be human is to be filled with the vastness of myriad relationalities, present and past. It is to be inherently and deeply connected to the entire world, seen and unseen, known and unknown. The nature of being is relationality, not autonomy. It is anything but nihilistic. In what follows I unpack these ideas some more.

Anatta: experiencing the emptiness of self

In my job as a lecturer in NUI Galway, I taught a module called 'Buddhism, Politics, Society', and in order to explain *anatta* to my students I usually told a story of my own experience as a student in the same university, then called UCG. In the second year of my BA degree,

I was particularly taken by lectures on the Scottish eighteenth-century Enlightenment philosopher David Hume and his 'bundle theory' of things. Our lecturer, a Franciscan friar, explained the concept by exemplifying something very mundane, a tomato. Did a tomato have an essence, he asked us. Might that be its colour? Its taste? Its shape? He requested that we identify and then imaginatively peel away all the qualities of a tomato in order to see if we might find an essence, a thing perhaps outside of colour, taste and shape that makes tomato precisely that and not onion, or aubergine. In words and with a gesture that I still vividly recall, he held his empty cupped hand up into the air and said that we would not find anywhere the 'shivering essence' of tomato. Our small exercise, he said, illustrated Hume's theory: we would not find the essence of tomato precisely because it did not have an essence. Rather, what we call 'tomato' is, according to Hume, a very particular combination, or a bundle, of many different qualities such as shape, taste, size, structure, texture and colour, all the characteristics we had suggested. Hume, of course, was not terribly interested in tomatoes but in offering a way of thinking about human life. As one of the early Enlightenment philosophers, he sought to challenge the dominant views about innate qualities of humans and the arguments from design for the existence of God. Just as the tomato has no essence, he said, humans too have no essence. What we experience is a bundle of sensations, our self being nothing more than our perceptions about those sensations and their causal relationships. Hume's position was revolutionary, undermining the authority of the Catholic Church, and his ideas were widely circulated at the time.

Inspired by this revelation, and convinced that I would indeed find my essence or my permanently abiding core, I decided to conduct a small experiment on myself. Though raised in the Catholic Church, I was no longer a Christian but I held fast to the idea that I had a soul, or some thing that was uniquely and permanently me, unchanging and particular to myself. The experiment was launched one morning as I made my way into that day's lectures. As I walked, I first identified and named and then mentally cast off various characteristics and qualities that seemed to gather around my identity. Could I do without my name? Yes. That seemed simple enough, no one needs a name to exist. What about things like my preferences in music? I could certainly exist without music of any kind: it was not essential to my identity. What about, then, my hair colour, the fact of body hair itself, my body shape, my limbs? What about my family background or the fact that I was a student of philosophy? Surely none of these constituted my essence? I mentally stripped them all away as I walked along and it seemed quite easy and enjoyable to be playing around with Hume's bundle theory. I imagined these superfluous bits of myself floating off in the canal that ran alongside my route, out to the Atlantic ocean. After some time, however, I very abruptly hit a very terrifying space. I confronted a complete nothingness. Emptiness. It seemed to me, devastatingly so, that 'I' was just a bundle of tags, habits, inherited beliefs, bodily bits, thoughts and memories, scraps of language and bucketloads of prejudices and emotions, all strongly felt but all very unstable. 'I' didn't seem to exist. It felt as if I had, in fact, annihilated myself on that sunny morning beside the canal. Having stripped away myriad qualities and parts constellating around my identity, there seemed to be nothing left at all. Much as I would hear the Tibetan teacher predict years later, I failed to locate my essence. What this amounted to, then, was a feeling that I didn't, in fact, exist. I was some kind of ghost. Empty.

The experience was, of course, deeply disturbing. Assuming that I was the only person who didn't actually exist, I kept this discovery to myself. No one else I knew seemed to be troubled by a similar absence and it didn't seem like something to own up to. My non-existence, moreover, seemed shameful, and naturally I worried a lot about it and feared others would somehow discover it too. Stuck still in a Judaeo-Christian worldview, it was not a cause for celebration or an exciting discovery. Coming to Buddhism years later, hearing the kinds of words spoken by the Tibetan monk, it became clear that neither my experience nor its outcome were unusual and certainly not shameful. I had gone down a path that Buddhist philosophy urges us along as the path to liberation. Had I then had access to that perspective, I might have appreciated that my experience had allowed me to see through the delusion of the 'self' as a permanent, essential and unchanging thing, and I might have found that there was, in fact, a much larger, richer world 'inside' me, a world that in Buddhism is considered the very ground of being.

For those new to Buddhism, these ideas often start to get tricky, as was evident with the Tibetan monk's audience. No one will contest the idea that we change, sometimes dramatically, from childhood into adulthood and into old age, but surely, it will be said, there is something that remains constant? We can observe this for ourselves in people we know well – a constancy that is particular to them. There must surely be an 'I', a stable entity that remains and resonates, even in the face of all the changes across a life course? If there is no such entity, then what holds everything together? Here, we come up against the limits of language. English, like all Indo-European languages, is structured around nouns (things that are distinct, have firm boundaries, as expressed by their name and the qualities we ascribe to them) and then verbs, adjectives and other modifiers: a crooked table; a mangy cat. Our language structure assumes that each thing, for which there is a noun, is entirely distinct from every other thing and that these things inhabit their world autonomously. It is hard for us to *think* crosswise as it may be hard to accept that, while nouns (table, cat) are very necessary for us to communicate meaningfully, they are just a construction of language, built on a shared meaning, but do not tell us the truth about the nature of the things. The way our language is structured and its influence on how we perceive the world doesn't easily accommodate Buddhism's claim that everything is in flux and everything arises in relationship to everything else, so that the identity of each and every thing is inseparable from the identity of each and every other thing.

With a little bit of imagination we can see its truth. If we break apart a table in our minds, we will find wood, perhaps hinges or glue, paint and varnish, so that in fact 'table' is made up of multiple other component bits, each with its own noun-name. The table would not exist without the carpenter or machinist who assembled it, the person who delivered the wood to the workshop, the oil barons whose oil fuelled her delivery van ... and on and on it goes. So 'table' exists of course, but only in relation to this vast, complex world involving economics, international trade, health and safety regulations, price controls and fashions in furniture styles. Thus, as with the tomato, the table has no essence but exists interdependently with many other forms, shapes, histories, places and beings. In Buddhism the same is true of each of us and of all sentient beings. Likewise, we are each, individually, physical, material beings with life histories, memories, identities, longings and desires, but what is illusory is the idea of a self as an unchanging, immortal essence.[127]

What I felt deeply during my experiment was the absence of essence, and having no other way of thinking about it, I experienced it as a devastating void at the core of my being. Two Zen teachers to whom I spoke for this chapter validated the experience of terror that can come with this insight, particularly if the person concerned is already feeling disconnected from the world. A student of one reported that she feared she had become psychotic during meditation when she felt the boundaries of her self – what she understood to be her self – dropping away.[128] It was as if she did not quite know where 'she' ended and the material world around her began. However, Buddhism suggests that this experience can be understood as a deep realisation that we are not what we think we are: that we are not our ideas, our habits and memories, and our behaviours. In these moments we can see, and really feel, that everything that constitutes our 'self' is flowing rather than static, ever changing, open and buoyant.

The image of a whirlpool illustrates this flux. A whirlpool is definitely something. We can recognise it, describe it, and know it to be different from a waterfall or other forms that water takes. But a whirlpool has no solidity as such and, depending on what is flowing downstream, it can be muddy and opaque, a mass of twigs and other materials, or made up entirely of whirling water. That student who imagined herself psychotic when she felt her boundaries 'drop away' was experiencing this lack of inherent solidity. Her thoughts and bodily sensations were changing in the same way that a 'whirlpool' changes. If we pay close attention we will see a constant flow of thoughts, ideas, memories and bodily sensations moving through us even though we spend our time trying not to be changed, trying to be immovable.[129] The student was somewhat untutored and felt deeply threatened by her experience.

Thus, while I, unwittingly, also experienced a foundational Buddhist idea, that of non-self, I did so outside of its necessary companion idea, that of 'dependent origi-nation': that nothing arises independently or from itself alone. Had I been equipped with a Buddhist worldview then, the outcome might have been rather different. I could have discovered that I was deeply connected. Instead of nothingness, I might have found every-thing.[130] But I was, like the tomato stuck in Hume's bundle theory, without access to any other perspective. A little learning is indeed a dangerous thing!

Buddhism thus invites us to give our 'thinking minds' a rest and instead to experience how we continuously bring forth this 'sense of me' and give it solidity, val-idating the idea that it has a separate and stable exis-tence. We are invited to explore, somatically, the identity project, our continuous attempts to turn ourselves into something solid, substantial and 'real'. We will see that this project begins at birth and continues through the multiple and multi-layered experiences we have from then onwards, not just the good ones (such as having lovingly attentive care-givers) but also the bad ones (such as having cruel, inattentive care-givers) and every-thing in between, and through which we shape a sense of self which we, in turn, believe to be the basis of an individual, distinct and stable personality. We may be-lieve in the soul as the entity that, in some delightfully mysterious way, holds our essence.

As a child, the idea that I had my own unique soul, something special inside me, was comforting. It served, however, a secondary function as an effective behaviour modification and disciplining system: each breach of the strict moral code (each sin or even the thought of sinning), I believed, left a smudge on that otherwise pristine soul and reparation was required to scrub it clean again. The concept of soul was thus imbricated with fear and anxiety and was one of the most powerful tools the Catholic Church had for keeping its flock in line. Yet, even as such an oppressive authority system has loosened its power, we are culturally reluctant to let go of the notion of soul; it serves some purpose for our self-understanding, is somehow necessary for the idea of an 'I'.

Existentialism explains our creation of a sense of 'I' as something solid and eternal by the fact that we simply cannot bear the idea that there is nothing stable and permanent at our core. We grasp onto the idea that there is an 'I' in order to escape the sense of lack and the 'trace of nothingness' in our being, including its relationship to the threat of death itself. We objectify ourselves, clutching onto something that is not itself containable: our consciousness. As the canopy of religion and religious-orientated life has faded in the West, the sense of inadequacy that is at our core is projected onto a need to fill up our lives with more in order to solidify this desired 'I'. We can do this in many ways, through fame, romantic love, money or technology,[131] all offering a way of filling up the absent presence and soothing our fears that we may not exist in any solid way. So what does Buddhism say? From the ontological start point of *anatta*, students of Buddhism are offered a systematic way of thinking about how this self gets shaped and brought forth. The explanation rests on the interplay of *skandhas*, a word translated, as we saw, into the English word 'aggregates' and of which there are five. The idea is that in each and every moment, in a process that is complex and often beyond our conscious awareness, these aggregates engage with each other to produce a sense of a self that we believe to be uniquely ours, our very own essence, isolated from each and every other person's essence and every other person and every other thing.

So how exactly do *skandhas* work and what are they? The first *skandha* relates to our form, or to our physical body. The second is our senses, to what we feel, smell, see, taste and hear. The third concerns how we think about or conceptualise everything, including what our senses register through the eyes or nose or tongue. The fourth concerns what is called mental formations: habits, prejudices and preferences, including our willpower and volition and all the human qualities such as pride, desire, hatred and greed. And finally, the fifth aggregate: consciousness. I like to think of the fifth as the conductor of the orchestra.

Caroline Brazier, a Buddhist psychologist, suggests that we think about the process by beginning, perhaps counter-intuitively, with the fifth *skandha*. This *skandha*, our consciousness, she says, captures the *outcome* of the process that is experienced through all the others, from our physical form, to gross feelings and emotions, to our conceptualisations about what is happening in any moment. It is in the realm of the fifth *skandha*, as outcome, that the idea of self emerges, and produces what she calls the 'self prison'. We can think about each *skandha* as constituting a different stage of a process whereby our perceptions, felt in the physical form, are given emotional power, are shaped by our habits, expectations and prejudices and are conceptualised by or in our mind. Our experience of the world at any moment, no matter how fleeting, is through this interplay of *skandhas* which creates and recreates the 'I' that has a history, is bolstered by memories, and seeks to reaffirm that history in every experience. She nicely captures the cycle as follows:

> Simply, we can say that how we perceive conditions how we react. How we react conditions the kind of mental structures we carry. The mental structures we carry then condition how we approach life. How we approach life conditions what we perceive. This pattern is a loop that reinforces itself constantly. Each of us continually seeks affirmation that we are the person who we have assumed ourselves to be. Situations that disturb this process are avoided or reinterpreted, and the self appears to become more substantial. What we need to bear in mind, however, is that this process is in origin a defensive one. Its effects are to limit our potential, to cut off possibilities for new action, and to tie up energy in the maintenance of this self-structure.[132]

Another way of putting it is as follows:

If we start with the raw material on which the mind is built, we see that our senses are the data we use for discerning, reasoning, and ultimately acting upon the world. The mind is where these senses merge, and it organizes the data in understandable bits, using memory as the template for recognition and orientation. We proceed forward by knowing what has already occurred in the past. Knowing is the mind's form of security, and it advances only under the assurance of its history. This knowing confines us to a fixed relationship with objects.[133]

This quote draws our attention to the 'self' therefore as a process of continuous creation and recreation within which our mind plays a powerful role. While it is instructive to break down the process into aggregates, in truth the process whereby we create our sense of self is not at all linear, nor easily broken down into clearly bounded stages. It is a lot more messy than that and, once we pay attention, we will see that, most of the time, we inhabit a world of emotions, sensations, thoughts, habits, ideas, memories, and so on, in endless movement. What these accounts draw our attention to is, firstly, this quality of impermanence, the constantly moving and changing inner/outer world of emotions, thoughts, sensations, memories, habit impulses that constitute how we are in the world and, secondly, our impulse to 'fix' a self in this flow: to extract a steady narrative that we then fix as the self.

When 2,500 years ago the Buddha first began to

articulate this view of the self, it was a dramatic challenge to the Hindu ideas then taken as unquestionable. In offering a different conception, he was obliged to counter the hegemonic views of the day, which he did through a systematic, point-for-point rebuttal of the justifications for the existence of a soul within Hinduism. The radicalism of his view is underlined by the fact that reincarnation (of souls) underpinned and sacralised the caste system of the time and the entire culture rested on the idea of a permanent entity that was particular to each person but which passed on after them as part of the cyclical nature of life. Buddhism's rejection of these ideas, and consequently their rationalisation of the caste system, required a lot of explaining then, and today still has relevance. Here is Olendzki's summarised take on the detailed defence offered by early Buddhism:

> The argument for the self taken on by early Buddhists included: *constancy*, the view that something unchanging underlay the perpetual flux of sensory and cognitive experience; *agency*, the felt sense of a person having the power to autonomously initiate action; *ownership*, the idea that all immediate experience was the intimate possession of a particular individual; *survival*, the widespread belief that an enduring personal pattern will be reborn after the break-up of the body; *responsibility*, the understanding that there must be a locus for the causal relations between a deed and a fruit; and *awareness*, the outlook that every individual is the centre of a locally generated field of experience which is assumed to have sacred origins.[134]

However, Buddhism asks us to directly experience what happens in our own bodies. Hence, students of Buddhism are invited to explore this whole messy process of flow and fix for themselves. Meditation practice is the primary site of this exploration, precisely, and powerfully, because it requires us to simply stop all physical activity, sit still and observe carefully. Beginning meditators will be invited to sit down and pay attention to what their mind does. It will, at the very least, reveal an ever-present flow of emotions and sensations, swirling about, rumbling alongside thoughts, themselves racing, sometimes uncontrollably. Present too will be memories, images, desires, all showing up with stories to tell, all wanting attention. It is not unusual for meditators to feel under siege by what their minds produce – jingles, earworms, repeated desires, old gripes never resolved. Peter Conradi, an English writer whose small book *Going Buddhist: Panic and emptiness, the Buddha and me* is a beautiful introduction to Buddhist thought, describes it thus:

> It can be shocking even to start to see how busy the mind is, constantly and inventively cooking things up. Most think we 'know our own minds'. Yet strange and hitherto unacknowledged thoughts approach like foreign armies marching over the brow of a hill, one after another. Thoughts can also have the speed of a waterfall, tumultuous, Niagara-like, seemingly unstoppable … thick, fast and churning … [A] common surprise for the meditator comes from seeing how many thoughts kidnap the thinker, taking him far away.[135]

A critical point here is that the mind is not separate from the 'I'. Rather, something called 'I' (as a separate entity) exists because the mind thinks it into creation.[136] And it does so time and time again, building onto memories and preferences, stories we tell ourselves continuously, responses that we have over and over again so that they come to be a 'truth'. Unless we take time, as Conradi says, we simply assume that we 'know' ourselves and that we are acting from self-knowledge and have total agency in all actions. The truth is that much of what we do is habit and a lot is compulsive.

The *skandha* model rests on a social psychology that speaks to the perennial condition of humanity, no matter what the context.[137] However, each of us creates our 'sense of me' inside place and time, history and culture and it is important to recognise that what results from the process is never the same cross-culturally or within cultures. Some societies are, in the Buddhist sense, manifestly more delusive than others because of the socialisation of particular norms, values and ideologies and through the enforcement of laws and institutions. Ideologically driven totalitarian societies demand of their citizens a very high level of uniform self-identity and promote enmity and violence towards out-groups. Similarly, and as we saw in the previous chapter, free-market capitalism glorifies an entrepreneurial acquisitiveness that subordinates ethics to the ideology of the market. We are very vulnerable to the circulation and propagation of social norms and values and, in particular, to workings of power, whether distal or immediate.

We may not even be aware of the way in which our sense of self is being shaped by these forces. The psychologist, David Smail, developed a social materialist explanation for much of the psychological distress he met when working in the British health service during the Thatcher era. He made the case that our attitudes and beliefs are not personal possessions, in the way that our body parts are, but are linked to and partially produced by a network of social forces that may stretch out to the most distant cultural powers.[138] Thatcherism brought psychological suffering as people struggled with the weakening of the social contract, and the sense they made of their experiences was heavily dependent on culturally defined meanings and explanations, in this case increasingly neoliberal values. Thus, he commonly met people experiencing what they believed was personal and professional failure because they were not achieving according to the values of this new market-orientated world.

Society can, for instance, nurture a restless, sensation-hungry and escapist kind of humanity, undermining and trivialising our capacity for ethics and compassion.[139] As I argue in this book, neoliberalism empties out relationality from the self in the same way that its economies empty out the social by denigrating the very idea of 'society' in favour of 'economy'. Thus when we think about delusions that we carry about the nature of self, the forms and extent of this delusion are also socially inherited.

So, in conclusion to the discussion of *anatta*, we can think about the self in Buddhism as an aggregate of aggregates, or a bundle of bundles, which, to our cost, we take for something substantial, permanent, stable and distinct from all other selves and beings. Thus we can think about the process involved here as 'selfing', whereby we create and recreate, in virtually every moment, a being that we believe is endowed with agency, permanence, constancy, responsibility, ownership, awareness and with some capacity to survive beyond death, much as Hinduism did at the time of the Buddha in relation to the soul. For Buddhism, this is the great delusion. Everything falls away, we get sick, our desires are ever shifting to ever-new objects, we die. However, in accepting impermanence we are freed up to live boisterously or quietly, whichever is our preference, but without the need to find, defend and validate a 'self'.

Pratityasamutpada: experiencing dependent origination

It may have become evident in the above discussion that it is quite difficult to speak of *anatta* (and the *skandhas*) without at the same time speaking of dependent origination. However, to try and separate them again for clarity, I will return to my experience of *anatta* by the canal in Galway. Had I had access then to Buddhist thought, how would the outcome have been different in terms of my conclusion that I was somehow void?

Had I known about the concept of dependent origination then, I might have understood that, while I experienced my self as empty, I might also have understood that I was *filled* with the entire world of my experiences since birth and before birth. I was by no means empty or void. In mentally breaking off the connection between myself and, for instance, my name as some kind of essential identity-maker, I failed to see that my given name was one rich and bountiful cause and condition of my existence, no less valid because of its instability in my identity or because it did not create a stable 'I'. Taking my name alone, I might have experienced myself as being one of many Wards – and Healys from my mother's side – with roots in rural east Galway farmland, Mayo towns and suburban Dublin, populated by ancestors who directly shaped my being through their genetic code and thus live on in me, but also as an inheritor of an ancient language and all its rich culture, with multiple layers of memories and connections, bound up with learning about place, history, and with the power of naming itself. I was fully and deeply connected to all of these, past and present. I carried their traces, coming together in my body in that particular instant, and they co-constituted who I was. I was (and am) dependently originated, not separate from any of those causes and conditions. My self is constituted thus by fathomless relationality, by the social. This is the ground of being, how things really are.

Sallie B. King puts it as follows:

> [W]e are constantly constructing ourselves by the choices we make, the food we choose to eat, the friends with whom we associate, the idea to which we turn. Clearly these choices are not and cannot be made in isolation. They exist as part of the great web of interdependence ... by and through our parents, the causal and conditioning of the air we breathe, the Earth we stand upon ... the love or abuse we receive from family, the ideas we learn from teachers ... the culture that gives us language and concepts, and so forth. We do not exist for a moment in isolation from all these things. We are like all other things in the world, being caused and conditional by others and causing and conditioning others in turn.[140]

We can think about this as follows: self is, at any one moment, filled with everything else in the field of experience of that moment. But that particular moment has been shaped by the near and distant past and by expectations and fears for the future. It is teeming with many lives. It is connected through memory, time, space, culture and language, through the material and natural worlds we are part of. It is never separate from any of this. Non-self, *anatta*, is a function of this interdependence; we cannot be correctly understood as separate selves.[141] We originate dependently and we cannot be without multiple others. We may, for instance, think that there is an 'I' that is taking decisions based on free will, but that 'I', and the decision taken, arises from causes (such as inherited or cultural values) and conditions (the immediate context) so that the decision does not, magically, emerge from an 'I' that is separate from all relationships around me.

Thus, the idea of dependent origination is inseparable from the theory of mind set out above. They are the flip side of the same coin. Irish psychiatrist Brendan Kelly puts it like this: perceived phenomena, including the idea of self, are entirely dependent on specific causes and conditions for their apparent existence and are thus without substance, permanence or, in a sense, independent existence.[142]

Citing a psychiatrist to shed some light on dependent origination is no coincidence. Buddhist thought has found a new footing in the West precisely because it mirrors contemporary neuroscientific and psychological approaches to understanding consciousness.[143] Indeed it has been argued that the Buddha may have been the greatest psychoanalyst of them all,[144] and dependent origination is remarkably akin to the scientific view that 'nothing happens by chance, or by divine decree. Everything happens because of a network of causes, and these causes can be discerned.'[145]

A key point of convergence is the idea, now accepted in medical science, that the brain is a thoroughly social entity. We are built for connecting with other humans so that it virtually makes no sense biologically to speak about individual brains. Though each of us has a distinct mass constituted by billions of brain cells, each one of those has about ten thousand connections to other brain cells and each is releasing hundreds of chemicals, all of which are interacting with and reacting to the environment. From birth and indeed before, our development is based on social cues, mirroring, and interactions with all of those around us. If deprived of human contact, an infant's brain will not develop or will develop badly. Purely at the level of biology, our brains are shaped by and grow through social interactions.[146]

In the past two decades an extensive dialogue has emerged between psychologically grounded approaches to understanding the self and Buddhism. Barry Magid, a New York based psychiatrist and Zen teacher, has done much to explore this terrain. There is great proximity, he says, between Buddhism's view that the self cannot be known as an essence, different from its manifestations, and current developments in psychology. The idea that the self does not exist as a separate, fixed entity, solely 'inside' the person, but is constituted relationally within an 'ever-changing self object or intersubjective field',[147] moreover, would find a welcome home in deep ecology and some strands of feminist thought, where a similar case is made for our ongoing inter-relationality, or our inter-subjectivity.

While thus foundational ideas about the nature of self are shared between Buddhism and humanistic or self-psychology, there is also much to be said about the beneficial practices that can flow from these ideas in terms of responding to our own suffering. Emphasising the deep webs of connection within which we all function

– though they may be ruptured – can be a powerful antidote to a suicidal urge when it, in turn, is a function of a constricted, isolated mental state. An appreciation of flux, the fact that change is inevitable, equally supports people who feel stuck in intractable situations.[148] If everything changes, then there are always possibilities. Nothing is predetermined.

Conclusion

What this discussion points to finally, and where this chapter would like to conclude, is the liberatory aspect of the Buddhist account of the self. Above, we saw how these ideas can be a helpful catalyst for change or for tolerance and survival in extreme psychological distress. In a more everyday sense, these ideas constitute the nexus of our freedom. Firstly, a Buddhist ontology frees us from the delusion that there is a self that has its own essence, distinct from every other person's essence. According to Buddhism, attachment to this idea of the self – and the need to defend and consolidate it with self-serving, self-aggrandising, self-protective actions and behaviours – is the root cause of human suffering. The burden of a belief in our own absolute reality is itself lifted and we are freed up to respond from a different set of values. Smith calls this the liberation of stepping out of self-deception.[149] However, secondly, it is in the surrender to what is actually there – dependent origination, the web of deep interconnectivity – that we can see and act out of no-self, and this is not, as is sometimes perceived to be the case in Buddhism, a transcendence above the human condition, but rather a full and wholehearted opening to the human condition, without that attachment to a self. It is, perhaps, more like a diving into the world and its messiness. Acting from emptiness means we can choose in each moment to respond to what is and to do so in a way that supports and validates our deeply social nature. Acting from emptiness is inherently pro-social.

From a Buddhist point of view, we have got it very wrong in the West, in our determined belief in some constant, autonomous entity at the core of each of our being. But it's not such bad news because we have the pleasure of seeing this delusion clearly, and in turn liberating ourselves from the suffering attached to trying to solidify and protect this 'self'. This chapter attempted to separate out the twin ideas of non-self and dependent origination but they are, as we saw, intimately related. The emptiness of all things consists in their meaningful interdependence. Realising the emptiness of things – that they have no essence – is the same as realising how each thing contributes to the meaning of all other things.[150] It is, as I said at the outset of this chapter, anything but nihilism.

In the same way that it's important not to be naive about the state, it is equally important not to be naive about Buddhism. In the West, we are easily seduced by 'orientalism': a fetishisation of all things Eastern, and Buddhism too is not immune from the romance. In the next chapter, I explore this by taking what might seem like a contrarian and extreme sidestep into a bleak chapter in Asian history, the Cambodian genocide. I do this to illustrate the manner in which a Buddhist culture and Buddhist ideas can be turned to such murderous extremes, thus illuminating our need to remain open to and critical of these ideas and all those that seem 'true' at any particular time. I also wish to draw from within the hard place of peace work in post-conflict and post-genocide Cambodia, the power and yet delicate complexity of the idea of non-self to help re-envision and rebuild a future. Ultimately, the story of Cambodia, as told in this book, is about the profundity of the social in the self.

Being Kind to the Khmer Rouge

S ome years ago I travelled to Cambodia for a research project on Buddhist peace work there. At the time, Cambodia was shaking off its dark past and presenting itself as a destination for international tourism and for investment by multinational capital. The noisy and colourful streets of the capital, Phnom Penh, were thronged with backpackers and high-end tourists, most of whom travelled to the ancient monastic sites, such as Angkor Wat, where they saw the dramatic manifestations of the commingling of religion, society and state in Cambodia's history. A large part of the country's attraction continues to be the richness and depth of its Buddhist culture, Buddha statues and symbols, tiny gongs and incense sticks all being part of the store of gifts and mementos those tourists carried back to their homes in Europe, the US or Australia. Though sadly I didn't have time for tourism – a series of interviews was lined up – I did meet some extraordinary people.

My interest in Cambodia arose, however, largely because of its dark past: the murderous and brutalising regime of 1975 to 1979, when the Maoist-inspired Communist Party of Kampuchea, known as the Khmer Rouge (KR), took power in a coup and almost immediately began killing its own people. It is estimated that about one quarter of the population was either killed or died from starvation or disease; that is, about 1.7 million people. Visitors to the grim former prison and torture centre Tuol Sleng, now a museum, learn that the killing continued right up until the last moments as the Vietnamese army advanced on the capital in 1979. The horrors of the KR regime are deeply disturbing, notwithstanding the somewhat mitigating prior context of decades of instability, including a civil war and the violent Cold War politics visited upon the country. Indeed, the international dimensions of KR power continued after the regime was felled, and after the Paris peace talks of 1991 that formally ended the conflict. Both the US and China supported the KR's claim to represent Cambodia at the United Nations right up until 1993.

It was, however, domestic dimensions of the KR regime that interested me. Since its early history, Cambodian culture and society was utterly steeped in Buddhist thought and practices and yet it gave birth to the KR genocide. While the KR leadership faced trial at a criminal tribunal, many supporters and cadre were now back in Cambodian society, living cheek by jowl with former victims and their families. The peace activists I wished to speak to worked in this fraught post-conflict context, grounding their work in Buddhism, towards healing past wounds, promoting reconciliation and preventing or resolving future conflict. My interest was initially sparked by a short article I read by NGO activist Ubasak Sotha Ros on both the limitations and possibilities of Buddhism to rescue Cambodia from the 'deep political hole' it had fallen into. The article set out a large agenda: monks needed to re-learn Buddhist philosophy, be trained in the right tools to incorporate spirituality into peace education, and be allowed to engage in social activism and conflict resolution. To counteract the possibility of continued political violence, the wider population, moreover, needed education in core Buddhist values of ethics, meditation and wisdom.[151]

I was intrigued to hear more about his analysis. Were the peace activists, monastics or otherwise, drawing from traditional Buddhism or working with a more contemporary version? What, if anything, made their activities specifically Buddhist? There were many tensions to be considered. For instance, the young Cambodian woman who assisted me with translating and other tasks had no doubt about where she stood. With no hesitation she told me that when she saw monks on the streets – they are hard to miss with their shaved heads and bright saffron robes – she turned away. They symbolised corruption, backwardness and an oppressive power structure manifest in their reliance on locals to provide for them. Neither she nor any of her friends had any interest in meditation or in Buddhism. She was very puzzled by my interest in them.

This chapter addresses this kind of contradiction in order to deepen our understanding of the relationship between the social and the self in Buddhism. It necessarily pushes forward another theme: the vulnerability of Buddhist thought to appropriation and exploitation. Earlier, we saw the exploitation of Buddhist symbols to sell happiness and the promise of spiritual insights. Buddhist concepts and language can be equally commandeered for more malevolent and treacherous purposes. But as argued by the peace activists I spoke to, this does not render those concepts invalid. As Buddhist teachers point out, misappropriation of ideas is something that we humans do. If you are already inclined to self-criticism, or to self-aggrandisement, driven unconsciously by habit, you might find yourself putting Buddhist thought to work to further punish yourself or further convince yourself of your superiority. Or if you are very adept, you might even pull off both at the same time.

To proceed, however, requires some background on the context of Cambodian Buddhist peace work. I firstly present a brief history of the KR regime and its relationship to Buddhism. I then move on to the efforts of peace activists to renew Buddhism for good use while keeping in mind that my focus is on notions of the self/other relationship, on the key idea of the emptiness of self.

The Khmer Rouge, genocide and Buddhism: a brief history

Cambodia has been a predominantly Buddhist country since the fifth century, and, by the thirteenth century, Theravada Buddhism was firmly established in the monarchy, in the monastic structures and among the population at large.[152] In a pattern found throughout Buddhist Asia, Buddhist practices and beliefs and monastic life were, throughout all these centuries, inseparable from civil and political life. Or to put it in a western formulation, there was no separation between church and state. Monasteries, known as wats, were the centre of social and cultural life in rural and urban Cambodia. Young men entered them as a matter of course, some remaining and some leaving again. During the colonial era, attempts by European powers to convert the population to Christianity were almost entirely unsuccessful, and the French colonial powers, in time, came to understand Buddhism as providing a set of ideas that facilitated passivity, or, in other words, acquiescence to colonial authority. King Sihanouk, a monarch who shared many of the presuppositions of his European tutors, endorsed the 'languid assessment' of the colonisers when he said of Buddhism in Cambodia that it was 'a sweet religion whose doctrines of resignation are marvellously suited to a tired people'.[153] Monks, however, were also involved in resistance movements against French rule, including violent actions, and historian Ian Harris posits the view that Buddhist-inspired nationalism was a 'fertile seedbed' for the germination of Khmer communism.

The origins of the Khmer Rouge date back to post-Second World War politics in Europe, when several young Cambodians, then studying in France, came under the influence of the French Communist Party and formed what became the Khmer Rouge. Its founding rhetoric espoused freedom of religion, but in practice the party was to ruthlessly attempt to eradicate from Cambodia what it considered to be reactionary religions, meaning not just Buddhism, but also Islam and Christianity. However, its relationship to Buddhism was, at the same time, somewhat complex. According to Harris, Khmer Rouge leader Pol Pot, and several other of its founders, had inevitably internalised Buddhist ideas such as those relating to enlightenment, disciplined personal transformation and rebirth, so that they made their way into the unique mixture of ideas that shaped and then constituted KR ideology and policy. Pol Pot's full-on attack on the concept of individualism, for instance, is a likely outgrowth of Buddhist values of non-self.

By the 1960s, as the party was building itself, with support from both the North Vietnamese Army and the Chinese Communist Party, it had begun to harshly criticise the traditional monastic structure. Its argument was that the monk population, believed to be around 70,000 at the time, was an economic burden on the country, especially on rural peasants who had to provide food and other supports as per the tradition. Moreover, the doctrine of karma came under assault as the KR believed that it produced an acceptance of inequality, oppressive social structures and, ultimately, a passive people. Such concepts belonged to feudal times, it was said, when people accepted their fate without question, and needed to be swept away. But many monks and former monks did support the party in its early years and encouraged peasants to join its ranks.

Any explanation for the Khmer Rouge's emergence and its brutality must be located in several violent crucibles. One was French colonialism itself and the nationalist resistance it elicited. Secondly, and much more critically, was the realpolitik of Cold War politics, referred to earlier. Cambodia did not achieve full independence from the French until 1953, but the social and political destabilisation of the previous decades continued when the USSR, China and the US, and their regional allies, competed for dominance in Asia in the decades after the Second World War. One cataclysmic outcome was the Cambodian civil war of 1970–5. Here, supported by the North Vietnamese, the KR pitted itself against the pro-US regime then in power in Cambodia. Swathes of eastern Cambodia bordering Vietnam were carpet-bombed during the Vietnamese–American War as the US attempted to wipe out the Soviet-backed North Vietnamese forces. However, despite the early alliance with North Vietnamese communists, the KR allied itself fully after 1975 with China and was thus supported by both the US and China in their opposition to the USSR's influence in Asia. It was China, then, that became the KR's main support following the coup in 1975.

It provided military advisers and military hardware, food and other forms of aid between 1975 and 1979 and its support continued, as we saw, even after the KR was toppled. To say that Cambodia's history is tragic is an understatement, and its factionalised power shifts and alliances, both domestic and international, in the mid to late twentieth century did not help. But what of Buddhism in this?

During the civil war, many monasteries had been destroyed and, on taking power in April 1975, the KR continued in this vein, albeit more systematically and ruthlessly, manifesting the ideological positions it had developed in exile in France, in opposition and during the civil war. Within a very short time, many senior monks were executed and others were forced to laicise and leave their monasteries. Alongside most of the population, they were put to physical labour in extremely difficult conditions in the countryside. Sacred books were burned and monuments and images were smashed. A telling slogan from the time advised, 'If you demolish a statue of the Buddha you will gain a sack of cement'. By the end of 1975, almost all monasteries were destroyed, closed or commandeered for other purposes, virtually eliminating Buddhist institutions and public practices from Cambodian life.

However, the KR regime drew on, and reworked for its own purposes, cultural ideas of Buddhist origin. Concepts such as self-reliance, renunciation of the self, the repudiation of individualism – all values in the pre-existing cultural modes of being – were put to murderous ends. The Buddhist notion of mental training was brought into service to improve the cadre's capacities to execute their fellow citizens. The pronoun equivalent of 'I' was discouraged in daily conversation – fitting neatly with the Buddhist repudiation of the idea of an abiding self. In translating the Marxist concept of 'dialectic materialism', the KR settled on the Khmer words for dependent origination, a perversion which, surely, was not coincidental. Where the Marxist idea naturalises conflict based on inevitable competing interests between classes, the Buddhist idea naturalises affective qualities and virtues such as compassion and generosity based on the irreducible interdependence of beings, human and non-human. While laying waste to Buddhist temples and the monastics, the KR made good use of Buddhist cultural values and philosophies to legitimise and empower its regime. Harris refers to this hybrid of extreme violence, communist ideology and Buddhism as a 'crypto-monastic' arrangement: a distinctive feature of the Khmer Rouge experiment.[154]

This syncretic blend offers an intriguing insight into the vulnerability of any set of ideas to hijacking but also underlines the importance of appreciating that in Asia, religious leaders, rituals and spiritual norms inevitably become involved with the apparatus of state. As emphasised by Harris, it is important not to see Asian Buddhism as outside of history or politics, belonging to some pure space, beyond corruption and manipulation.

Buddhist peace work after genocide

Given this, then, how do activists return to Buddhist ideas to rebuild Cambodian society and encourage the development of what my interviewees called a 'culture of peace': an understanding that 'peace' meant not just the end of conflict, such as mediated by the Paris Accord of 1991, but extended non-violence into public and private life, from interpersonal relationships to economic development.

One of those I interviewed during my trip was a very poised, elderly woman called Tey Sambo, who worked as a programme officer for UNESCO after the peace accords, mostly in rural communities where large groups of former KR supporters or members and their families had been 'returned'.[155] Her motivation for the work arose because of a desire to assist in the post-conflict resettlement of the KR but also because she had a personal desire to understand how such extreme violence could spring up.

Some time into the interview, Tey Sambo located herself in the dark history. Her family – middle class, urban and educated – was precisely the social group that the KR targeted first for killing, and indeed she listed off all those belonging to her who had been murdered: her parents, siblings and many wider family members. She escaped death only because she had been transferred by the KR to the north of the country.

When I asked her what guided her, as a Buddhist peace activist, her response stopped me dead in my tracks.

Without any hesitation she said, 'We have to be kind to the Khmer Rouge.' This unexpected answer was both chilling and very affecting, and during the interview, I stumbled to make sense of it. Could someone whose family had been virtually wiped out really wish to show kindness towards the genocidaire? It is conceivable that, given time, we might let go of our desire to inflict terrible pain and misery on the KR. We might accept that the place for them was indeed at the tribunal, which was then, with excruciating slowness, trying the KR leadership. We might be willing to put aside our desire for revenge, trust due process and learn to live with the complex moral and emotional consequences of a civil war. But to argue for *kindness* towards all who were part of the killing was a different order of response.

As Tey Sambo spoke further, I saw in her stance shades of the pragmatic long-view that might be expected of a UNESCO employee working towards a culture of peace. Although perpetrators of genocide, the KR were included in the talks that led to the Paris peace accords in recognition that their acquiescence was necessary for the violence to end, without compromising on the case for their prosecution for crimes against humanity and other crimes. Such an approach, logically and fairly, says 'yes' to judicial processes to try and to punish those responsible for killing, and says 'no' to revenge and to score-settling acts that merely displace and perpetuate conflict.

Members of the families that Tey Sambo worked with had been deeply indoctrinated from an early age.

She discovered that, although the war was long over, the wounds were 'still inside'. Many were still KR in form, in their often-violent language, their dress and their way of thinking. All the while praising Pol Pot, they explained the absence of choice as contributing to their support of the regime. Inevitably, they faced the possibility of revenge from the surrounding population and many still had arms hidden away, but easily available, should they be required. Moreover, they feared punishment in a future life, as they believed that their terrible actions would result in a grim existence next time around.

Tey Sambo's stance was not to 'blame' the KR families but to offer them kindness. She worked to bring a disposition of compassion towards their plight. She understood, moreover, that they were not apart from Cambodian culture or from non-KR Cambodians. The KR came from within Cambodian culture at a particular place and time, given particular causes and conditions. Hence, while certainly KR leaders and commanders should face the full brunt of the special tribunal, Cambodians needed not revenge or further aggression, but kindness. Showing kindness allowed trust to develop between Tey Sambo and the families, and trust was sorely missing in post-conflict Cambodia. To illustrate, she told me of several times when she was accepted as a mediator in very volatile situations which had the potential for direct violence. Her interventions diffused the conflict, but just as importantly, they had a generative impact in terms of social capital, or trust. Her job was not just to resolve individual grievances (though that may have been what was presented immediately) but to restore the protagonists' understanding of themselves as intimately connected to the other – in this moment a KR-family member, in that a police officer linked to the other side – and more widely to restore an understanding of the precariousness of the human condition.

Hence Tey Sambo's commitment to kindness sprang from something more than pragmatism, an impressively deep humanitarianism or an ability to see that the KR families were themselves victims of the regime's violence. Its deep root lay in the Buddhist idea of dependent origination – the view of the self and other – and from the ethics or actions that flow from this state. Though in an extreme context, her approach points to the ethical aspects of Buddhist thought and its irreducibly social understanding of the self. She saw beyond the facts of the genocide and its destructive legacy and into something more perennial. Her response, though likely not easily come to within herself, drew out the possibility of generosity, forgiveness and a profoundly humane framework for peaceful reconciliation in Cambodia.

A second interviewee, former monk Heng Monychenda, spoke in a similar way of a project led by his organisation, Buddhism for Development. After the Paris peace accords, though the KR was 'reintegrated' physically, the emotional and mental reintegration required for reconciliation was missing. The whole of Cambodian society was fractured by a lack of trust and yet people had to live together again without resorting to the kind of violence that was, at this moment, still present. Out of this arose the Peace and Development Volunteers (PDV), a trained squad of locals, selected by their communities in a process that was itself democratic to serve as voluntary community mediators. Young men and women from both KR and non-KR communities were schooled together in human rights, Buddhist thought and community development principles. They relied on recognition of Buddhist ontology and ethics, absorbed by Cambodians even if, during the KR period, profoundly violated. With the idea of dependent origination, the idea of self as irreducibly social and relational, comes kindness and compassion. None of these concepts need to be taught anew to Cambodians, he explained. Rather, the PDV's work was to draw these out as living tools and show their efficacy to solve problems and to find a peaceful and fair way through conflict. Like Tey Sambo, he too offered examples of the power of this approach to diffuse and restore and, critically, normalise the conflict resolution skills inherent in Buddhist thought.

What may be hard to understand is how all of these actions are distinctly Buddhist. They seem to share much with other forms of peace-building or deep humanitarianism. Indeed, throughout my interviews, I was bedevilled by the question: what is distinct about what is going on here?

Many of those I spoke to used the term 'spirituality' when describing their work and sometimes in surprising ways. One spoke at length about the need for monks to be trained in spirituality – by which he meant not merely learning off sutras and rules – so that they could engage better and more authentically with Cambodian society. It became clear to me, but only after some time, that the key to understanding Buddhist peace-building was the understanding of spirituality and its relationship to ideas about the self.

In our western minds, we tend to think of 'spirituality' in a dualistic fashion: relating to the transcendent in opposition to the material. Left-leaning thinking in particular has given the 'spiritual' short shrift, being concerned primarily with the materiality of inequality, poverty and the workings of capitalism. Moreover, we tend to associate the 'spiritual' with ideas of the soul, a concept often repudiated by left-leaning thought. As we saw in a previous chapter, however, nothing in Buddhism supports the idea of a soul as understood in Abrahamic religions: something unique, permanent and abiding. Buddhism argues that we are irreducibly social, necessarily intimately, and dependently, connected to all others.

In Buddhist thinking 'spirituality' is not understood dualistically, standing against the 'secular' or 'material' or 'practical', but rather refers to the many practices with which Buddhists intentionally develop their insight, concentration and virtues such as compassion, kindness, equanimity and non-violence[156] in the context of the emptiness of self. The classical Buddhist term used is *bhavana*, the idea of the cultivation of virtues and mental states which arise or are available to us precisely because of dependent origination and non-self. Hence the prescription that Cambodian monks needed education in this worldview and not just in the recitation of verses and in the rules of the monastery.

But how does this understanding of spirituality affect what the PDV or Tey Sambo or the other Buddhist peace activists do? This requires a little further unpacking. The *sine qua non* of Buddhism is the reduction of suffering. Most of our suffering is caused by our tightening up around our notion of an enclosed separate self, causing both ourselves and others to suffer, manifest in a range of responses from low-level rudeness to the extremity of genocide. Practitioners of Buddhism seek continually to loosen up their attachment to self, to narrow views, to ego, and then to expand outwards in an all-inclusive way. This translates, for instance, into an idea of never turning away, whatever it is we meet or come in contact with. According to Buddhist understanding, then, every perspective on life is only a partial, experiential realisation of truth. The task, however, is not thus to try and gather together as many different realisations in the hope that they will, together, amount to something called 'the truth'. Rather, by getting inside a number of perspectives, we realise the partiality of each, including, most particularly, our own perspective. That recognition allows a loosening up of our own view, a necessary step towards grasping the full perspective.[157] In conflict-resolution terms, non-self is the ground on which such a shifting of perspectives can occur, a loosening of rigidities and tightness.

Recall here that Tey Sambo's work in promoting a culture of peace was motivated by the need to reduce the potential for conflict between returnees and the non-KR communities. In this goal, she was no different from most peace workers. But she was also motivated by a desire to get to know those who had participated in such violence and to fully understand them and their actions. This was, in Buddhist terms, an intention from spiritual practice: the desire to know for herself and to get close to those who killed or supported the killing of her family, neighbours, friends, fellow citizens. This getting close was both physical and operational (peace workers are obliged to go to hard places) and informed by Buddhism's commitment to an all-inclusive orientation to the world. She did not distance herself from them through professional guidelines or other strategies nor did she seek to present a judgemental or punishing face. Rather, she sought to expand and cultivate her own capacities for kindness and compassion even as they spoke with violence or praised Pol Pot. And although she didn't say this and I did not (foolishly and regretfully) ask her about it, I suspect that the kindness she showed to the KR families brought some resolution and healing for herself. I was deeply impressed at her resilience and her capacity to speak with compassion about the KR families. According to Heng Monychenda, PDV volunteers found also that while they successfully defused violence and eased community life, their own growth and expansion as Buddhist practitioners deepened. Their peace work 'outside' was not separate from the cultivation of peaceful qualities within themselves. They were one and the same. In this, the PDV's work was a spiritual practice.

Another way of thinking about all of this is through the Tzu Chi movement, a Taiwan-based Buddhist charitable organisation that provides free medical care. While donors are conventionally considered the benefactors, the organisation stresses that they are also beneficiaries. Their needs are met – not ego needs, but the need to be integral to something bigger and more bountiful than their small self. Participants are instructed that in immersing themselves in acts of giving, the sense of a separate self who is doing the giving will fall away and they will feel a constituent part of the greater natural whole, the unfolding process, the giving and taking that is life.[158] Giving, of self or one's resources, becomes a spiritual practice that is not about ego-need; peace work becomes a spiritual practice that opens up the space for the full expression of dependent origination.

Conclusion

This chapter treated a pretty hardcore theme – genocide – in its relationship to foundational Buddhist ideas. As we saw, the Khmer Rouge artfully exploited Buddhist ideas of renunciation of 'self' to promote extremely violent communalism in which various selves were considered of no human worth and valued instead for their potential as 'fertiliser' – to cite one of the expressions of the regime. Pushed to its extreme, and not balanced with other companion ideas, the basic idea of non-self can indeed be brought into service of murder in a truly degraded and nihilistic manner.

Sadly, we find similar appropriation elsewhere. During Japan's imperial war effort, Buddhist ideas of mental training and concentration were used to train soldiers required to engage in acts of extreme violence for the state.[159] Recently in Sri Lanka, during state genocide against the Tamil minority, a fifth-century Buddhist text, known as the *Mahavamsa*, was used to support a 'just war' against that minority. More recently still, in Myanmar (formerly Burma), the principle of non-violence, *ahimsa*, was reworked to justify genocide against a Muslim minority, the Rohingya. A monk named Ashin Wirathu – a man previously jailed for hate speech – told a public gathering that only the military could protect 'our country and our religion'. He later told the *New York Times* that if the International Criminal Court were to investigate crimes against the Rohingya he would 'hold a gun'. Another monk, Sitagu Sayadaw, committed the community of 400,000 Buddhist monks to supporting the military.[160]

But as always, the story is complex. While in Cambodia, I read a newspaper article about Burmese monks 'seething with rage' over the army crackdown against pro-democracy protestors, and a group called the All-Burmese Monks Alliance supported the pro democracy marches.[161] Equally, some Sri Lankan monks refused to support the campaign against the Tamils. Moreover, as in Cambodia, context is important. In Sri Lanka, account must be taken of the way unemployment, an entrenched pattern of agricultural expansion, and competition between political parties, overlaid with the power of an urban privileged elite, fuelled ethnic conflict.[162] In Burma/Myanmar, the military elite has run the country directly and indirectly for several decades. In these situations, Buddhism mingled with cultural values and norms so as to be inseparable from them, to help shape the vast interplay of causes and conditions.

But as we have seen in this chapter, Buddhist ideas offer a radical, though challenging, path even in places of extreme violence and even when some of those ideas have been part of the problem. The Cambodian peace-makers whom I met drew from the solid ground of an endlessly generating idea, not shared in peace activism in Asia or elsewhere. And that is the radical account of the self and the ethics that flow from it. It is this, I argue, that provides a deeply sustaining position on which to build a future-orientated vision for how we might live together without destroying the environment, each other, our collective resources and our sanity. It is this that distinguishes Buddhist activism from that of others.

As we have also seen in this chapter, Buddhism did not save Asian countries or their minority populations from extreme violence. It is tempting to conclude that the problem was an unmodernised Buddhism bound to powerful hierarchies, untouched by notions of human rights and equality. Indeed, both Cambodian monks I interviewed, Venerable Yos Hut and Venerable Nhem Kimteng, argued that a reinterpretation of karma was essential because its traditional equating with 'fate' meant blind acceptance of authority and encouraged passivity. Notwithstanding this, as we will see in the next chapter, Buddhist ideas are equally vulnerable to exploitation in high modernism also, in this neoliberal era, and it is to this that I now turn.

Why (Some) Mindfulness is Part of the Problem

It cannot have escaped anyone's attention that we have sanctified mindfulness as the miracle cure for virtually every conceivable human difficulty: problems with work colleagues, in personal relationships, career path confusion, mental and emotional health problems, in friendships, for children who can't pay attention, and, in a most recent manifestation that I came across in an Irish newspaper, problems with our sex lives.[163] In the last decade or so, mindfulness has penetrated our workplaces, where it is sold to employers as a tool to improve work efficiency and to reduce absenteeism, and to employees as a means to enhance our 'soft skills' for career advancement.[164] For good measure, mindfulness is often offered as a reliable defence against future unknown problems, a guaranteed insurance cover. Most controversially, perhaps, mindfulness is now incorporated into military training in the US and in other armed forces.[165]

Yet just twenty years ago, the idea of teaching mindfulness to six-year-olds or of hosting mindfulness in boardrooms would have been greeted with quizzical amusement. An Irish Zen priest I know, who lives in Japan, was puzzled some years ago while back on holidays. What is this 'mindfulness' thing? he asked. Mindful eating, mindfulness for teachers, mindfulness weekends: every day, the media extols the virtues of mindfulness. Buddhism is about 'unfilling' the mind, he said, why do people want their minds full? His puzzlement was not solely because of unfamiliarity with the word 'mindfulness' but also because, while the concept was presented as, somehow, Buddhist, no equivalent phenomena existed in Japan, a Buddhist country.

Some of his confusion arose from the challenge of cross-cultural translations. The term 'mindfulness' is commonly offered in English as a translation of the Pali word *sati*, which refers to a faculty of awareness, or a spiritual faculty. *Sati* connotes a mind that is active in a way that accords with the kind of spiritual practice explored earlier in relation to Cambodian peace activists. There is extensive debate among experts about the origin and precise meaning of the term *sati*, as Buddhism, and all of its conceptual luggage, made its way across Asia and, eventually, to the West. If you look up the word *sati* on Wikipedia, you will encounter a long discussion of Buddhist philosophy, though you may end up more confused as the experts have lots to say, sometimes in disagreement with each other.

At the heart of all of these discussions is, however, agreement that although *sati* may be interpreted with some differences within the various Buddhist traditions, within all it is inseparable, and ultimately indistinguishable, from both Buddhist ontology and ethics. In other words, the development of that awareness, or of that spiritual faculty (*sati*), is both foundational to Buddhism and cannot 'stand or sit alone' without interrelated ideas about the development of character, the cultivation of generosity and other virtues, the refinement of ethical sensitivity and the day-to-day activation of compassion.[166] The worldview within which all of this – virtues, ethics, character development – makes its meaning is founded on dependent co-arising, the emptiness of self. Hence, whether Buddhists speak about meditation, concentration, awareness, attention or bare attention, they are speaking of only one component of Buddhist cosmology. Mindfulness is Buddhism's way of keeping us attuned to the reality that we are irreducibly interconnected, that there is no 'self' to defend or consolidate, and from this insight flows ethics whose purposes are to reduce suffering. Thus, ontology, ethics and practice: all are one.

Yet, as we will see in this chapter, the mindfulness that we have sanctified has, to various degrees, extracted itself from that worldview and has become part of the problem that is the neoliberal subject. However, I wish to make the case for some nuance. Mindfulness is employed beneficially in western psychological traditions, including psychotherapy, to very powerful effect. In the hands of an experienced facilitator, it can help liberate us from deeply ingrained thought patterns that so often get us into trouble. Science supports claims about increased emotional stability and increased well-being as outcomes of mindfulness interventions.[167] Criticism seems churlish, thus, and more so given the many very honourable people committed to mindfulness. I met such people some years ago on a ten-day Mindfulness-Based Stress Reduction (MBSR) training course in an off-season County Wicklow hotel. It was a profound and very moving experience. Participants had come from all over the world and many – some of whom were Buddhist practitioners – were keen to bring the skills to community-based or educational settings, recognising that what happens in our minds *is* important and that greater awareness of mental or cognitive processes is an unmitigated good for human flourishing.

But a tension was evident. It became clear that there were also participants determined to speedily complete the entire training, of which this was just a preliminary step, in order to work in the corporate sector where, it was reported, large wads of money were available. The distinction I draw here is not between intended sites of work for trainees, one 'pure' and the other 'impure', but between the models of mindfulness held by trainees. One was close to the original idea of *sati* and one had travelled very far from it. For the latter group, mindfulness was simply a tool without the need of ontology or ethics. For the former, mindfulness was *sati*.

Many have written about the *sati*-less phenomenon, some offering the alternative term 'McMindfulness'.[168] While I draw on those critiques here, my purpose is solely to explore the manner in which what appears as somehow Buddhist, or is assumed to be Buddhist, may end up in fact producing, both materially and ideationally, that which Buddhism seeks to mitigate: a self that is separate, autonomous, a resource to be managed towards its own advancement and consolidation. In so doing, along with the happiness industry and the wellness industry, it has become a form of psychopolitics under neoliberalism, disciplining us into becoming good neoliberal subjects while being sold to us as a liberatory vehicle. Mindfulness has become, in the words of one of its harshest critics, a religion of the self, apolitical and evangelised, avoiding moral enquiry and reluctant to consider a version of the social good. It has become a form of capitalist spirituality.[169]

So here I want to be really clear: what I am critical of in these pages is this *sati*-less version of 'mindfulness' – something sheared from Buddhist thought, stripped of its necessary other parts and presented, usually with a high purchase price, as a panacea and a miracle cure for many woes and ills. It is sold as a product that gets you the outcome you want, be it better sex, greater clarity about your life's purpose, or calmer children. Yet this *sati*-less iteration still draws on Buddhist images and symbols, often makes use of terms like 'ancient teachings' that have come to us from 'the East' and is commonly suffused with claims about spirituality. Moreover, partly because of these narratives, mindfulness is widely perceived in the public realm to *be* Buddhism. Like many practitioners of Buddhism, I have frequently felt a good deal of anxiety about this travesty. The much-cited comment by Marxist social theorist Slavoj Žižek that Buddhism has become a handmaiden of capitalism bears a sting! Thus, critique is necessary, whether this *sati*-less mindfulness is presented in the boardroom, the clinic or the workplace.

In what follows, then, I present a brief explanation of mindfulness in Buddhist thought, and go on to present some of the key critiques in the scholarly literature of the apparently happy marriage of a *sati*-less mindfulness with neoliberalism.

Mindfulness and Buddhism

So where is the original account of mindfulness found in Buddhist thought and how is it conceived? Whatever form of Buddhism, whether modernised or more traditional, whether practised in Asia or in Ireland, they all share a common foundation known as the four noble truths. This states: 1) that we all suffer, 2) that there is a common origin to our suffering, 3) that we can diminish or halt our suffering and 4) that there is a way, or a path, to do this. I have come to like the interpretation of this four-part insight by Zen priest and poet Norman Fischer, who in a recent book breathes into it very fresh life. He emphasises the role for our imaginations, including our capacity as humans to hold paradox, to work with the 'impossible' and to see what is hidden or obscured from us. The four noble truths, he says, offer the following statements about what it means to be human:

> *Suffering*: all conditional existence is characterised by dissatisfaction and suffering.
>
> *Origination*: dissatisfaction and suffering originate in the failure of our imagination to see things as they truly are.
>
> *Stopping:* we can stop suffering by opening our imaginations to the truth of how things are and enter the peace of nirvana.
>
> *Path*: the way to effect this opening is through the practice of the Buddhist path of right conduct, right understanding and right cultivation of mind and heart.[170]

Thinking about the four noble truths and their relationship to mindfulness, it is important here to note, again, that, as set out in the third truth (stopping), our suffering arises because we fail to see or fail to act on the truth of our dependent origination. Not surprisingly, then, the medicine for our suffering, accordingly, is to turn back towards and embrace that ontological condition. The path to doing that, set out in the fourth noble truth, names mindfulness (*sati*) along with the other factors listed above in Fischer's interpretation. So what specifically is this path to less suffering?

For Zen Buddhism, mindfulness belongs on that path as one of six characteristics or abilities, called *paramitas*, that we all have by virtue of our human condition but which require cultivating or practising with, over and over, throughout our lives. Here, mindfulness is the door to the cultivation but is also the cultivation. Each *paramita* is essential to a Zen Buddhist practice so that mindfulness exists in an interrelated alliance with the four *paramitas* that can be considered 'codes of conduct' (they being: generosity, patience, ethics and joyful effort) and with the sixth *paramita*, which is wisdom. The first four *paramitas* may be considered as commonplace virtues – we all aspire to being generous and patient, for instance – while mindfulness (number five) and wisdom (number six) suggest a more spiritual or mystical frame of reference and call for the kind of effort beyond the normal course of our daily lives. All together the *paramitas* can be understood as defining a way of life, most definitely not a place to get to, so that they produce a kind of paradox: there's nowhere to arrive at, but we must keep trying anyway.

Before moving on, it is important to identify that mindfulness is usually described as having two elements. These are *samatha* (tranquillity) and *vipassana* (insight), or a receptive attention and a directive attention.[171] The former (*samatha*/receptive) involves creating conditions that allow the mind to become quiet and either bringing our concentration to bear on a single object, such as breath, or simply allowing our minds to rest, without having to have any particular focus. In Zen this is called focus-less meditation: we don't have to look at a candle flame, real or imagined, or count our breath. In *vipassana* (directive) we start to actively direct our attention while sitting. For instance, we may pay close attention to what physical sensations arise alongside emotions. We are likely to see patterns, such as the arising of physical heat and discomfort in the body when we experience the emotion of anger. Through this practice, if done often enough, we will discern a very particular truth: that all thoughts, emotions, feelings and sensations pass, all are impermanent, and that we can, with sustained practice, relinquish our attachment to various stories (thoughts, ideas) that we hold inside our heads and that are held in our physical bodies as physical sensations such as agitation, restlessness, a tightening of muscles in the gut, or sleepiness. As with *samatha*, we are in the realm of deeply somatic experiences. We get 'out' of our heads and into our physical bodies. We learn, over time, how to relinquish or transmute darker emotions and feelings without, importantly, clinging to lighter ones. In the Zen tradition, we learn to allow everything to be present, to include everything that arises. This is not a process of chasing away undesirable thoughts or feelings; it is, rather, about not clinging to anything, whether joyful and bright or difficult and dark. Through such sustained practice, the nature of the human condition is revealed to our consciousness. That is, in brief, the condition of impermanence, the emptiness of self and the profound sense of unsatisfactoriness that characterises how we approach, and live in, the world.

Stephen Batchelor, a long-standing practitioner writer and a proponent of something he calls 'secular Buddhism', describes his first *vipassana* experience and the direct insight it gave him into the fragility of the human condition:

> Without relying on any deities or mantras ... without having to master the intricacies of any doctrine or philosophy, I vividly understood what it meant to be a fragile, impermanent creature in a fragile, impermanent world. The mindfulness sharpened my attention to everything that was going on within and around me. My body became a tingling, pulsing mass of sensations. At times when I sat outside, I felt as though the breeze were blowing through me ... [A]t the same time, there was a deep stillness and poise at the core of this vital awareness.[172]

Clearly, this kind of insight speaks of a deep, embodied experience of a mature practitioner. Whole books have been written on what precisely happens in a meditation practice. In the everyday, most meditators sit and stew in an often-seething mess of emotions and in a cascade of rampaging thoughts – and with physical discomfort, to boot. Insights as to impermanence may themselves be pretty impermanent when, say, the same thought returns again and again, demanding our attention and creating solidity for itself: I am real and I need attention now! Most of the time, practitioners do not have such luminous experiences as described by Batchelor. Sitting can be very mundane: simply allowing thoughts to be quietened or allowing the body to experience intensity or unpleasantness without leaping up, swearing or doing any of the things we might normally do to distract ourselves. However, as this book is not a guide to meditation – plenty such books exist – my task is but to note some key points about *sati*, many of which will be returned to later.

Before moving on, there is the question as to what is distinct, if anything, about *sati*, given that meditative and contemplative practices are found in all the great religious traditions and outside of them. In its origins in Asia and as it evolved, Buddhism developed in a distinct way, one that requires instruction, discipline and development. For many in the West, a challenge of Buddhism is that it asks us to do a lot of 'nothing' but in a highly disciplined and sustained way and with a very particular orientation of mind. If a beginner, we will be instructed, sometimes in minute detail, in how to sit, where to place our hands, how to fold our legs and what to do with our eyes. We are then required to sit upright in this yogic posture and remain still with quiet breath and (ideally) an open awareness for prolonged periods. We will be encouraged to do this with others, following a schedule that includes collective rituals. In classical Buddhism the physical form we inhabit in meditation is likened to that of a tripod. The body is perfectly in balance, with both knees and the buttocks forming the three tripod tips, solid and stable. But the tripod metaphor also refers to the fact that meditation is one 'pod', ethics another and wisdom a third. We might suggest that we need meditation in order to support our ethical conduct. Or we could say that when we sit meditatively, ethics and understanding flow into our lives. Or we could say that understanding of the true nature of being is the core and meditation is necessary to allow this deep understanding arise. In truth they are simply different ways of thinking about the necessity of all three. It is as if they are one and the same.[173]

I would also like to raise here a further important point when thinking about *sati*. Though practitioners often sit on their own at home, the very notion of *sati* is saturated with an idea of the social. This idea is often captured with reference to what are called the 'three jewels' of Buddhism: Buddha (the person) the dharma (the teachings) and the sangha (the collective, the community). Anyone wishing to experience sustained practice will usually find some sangha with which to sit, and find that all their engagements with that community are filtered through *sati*. Monastics sit for many hours every day, as if solitarily confined in their individual bodies, but they live communally and, as should be clear by now, the wisdom of what they do and cultivate is that they themselves are 'empty' and at the same time full of each other and the world. We can think about mindfulness then as a collective practice that inevitably and necessarily unites practitioners towards manifesting a social ethic.

It is this practice of sitting and paying attention in a particular way and with a particular worldview that provided the foundation for the mindfulness that is now commercialised and reduced to a self-help technique, what I have come to call a *sati*-less commodity. In the next section I trace briefly the emergence and growth of that cottage industry.

How mindfulness became a 'thing' in the time of neoliberalism

The origins of the current mindfulness movement are customarily located with Jon Kabat-Zinn, a Boston-based practitioner of Tibetan Buddhism and medical scientist who wondered about a translation of his meditation practice into a medical setting, specifically to mitigate chronic pain. Clinical trials concluded very promisingly. The practice of sitting and paying very close attention to what was happening in their bodies and minds seemed to help those with chronic pain to cope better and live better lives. Kabat-Zinn subsequently developed a series of steps and interventions called MBSR, or Mindfulness-Based Stress Reduction, the programme that constituted the training I partici-pated in in County Wicklow. An offshoot, called MBCT, Mindfulness-Based Cognitive Therapy, evolved, using the techniques to help those suffering from depression. It was developed by two English psychologists and academics, Mark Williams in Oxford University and John Teasdale at Cambridge University. Both models were supported by a massive research industry as mindfulness spread and its usefulness to, for instance, boost the immune system, decrease anxiety and irritability, reduce stress including hypertension, and reduce the impact of serious conditions such as cancer and drug and alcohol addiction, was evidenced by further research.

So what is the problem with all of this? Ron Purser, perhaps the most ardent critic, points out that in 2019 'McMindfulness' was a 4 billion dollar global industry backed up with thousands of books, CDs, programmes and other purchasable items. It has become a massively successful product and, for him, its success has largely to do with its 'fit' with the individualistic and entrepreneurial ethos of neoliberalism, facilitated by the stripping away of the original ethical framework. It is not that clinicians, psychologists and others set themselves up to lubricate neoliberalism, but, partly, the frameworks that they bring to mindfulness (individual suffering, individual pain) were not set up to understand interdependence and the social aspects of the self. In the therapy room, there is a client and a clinician; in the hospital, there is the clinician and the person with chronic pain. In other words, in as much as western medicine and psychology has adopted mindfulness, it translates it into its ethically neutral, individualistic forms of intervention.[174] If the intention of neoliberalism is, as Purser believes, to destroy collective structures, then mindfulness, wittingly or unwittingly, facilitates this. We can suggest that, in absenting the moral foundation found in *sati*, this western version of mindfulness has opened itself up to being captured by capitalism, and many have gained from the capture. Headspace, a super-successful mindfulness app established by a young English man who had practised Tibetan Buddhism, is estimated alone to be worth $250 million a year.[175]

Purser's critique is uncompromising and short on nuance. It is also informed by the US context, and much of what he identifies may not be appropriate for what has happened elsewhere. His work sheds light, however, on how the phenomenon evolved. For this, we need to delve a little deeper into precisely what happens when we bring what in MBCT is called 'mental training' to bear on ourselves. How does it alleviate depression, stress and anxiety or the impact of, say, cancer treatment? And how precisely does it fit with neoliberalism? I focus on the MBCT practices developed to both prevent negative feelings from spiralling downwards into prolonged periods of exhaustion, unhappiness and depression, and to reduce the risk of repeated bouts for those suffering from depressive illness.[176]

MBCT in essence is a cognitive therapy that utilises mindfulness to address and modify what can be considered dysfunctional thinking. It works by training us to be highly aware of our thoughts, feelings and emotions and to not attach value judgements to them, rather to create a distance between them and ourselves within which we can, among other things, open up choice as to how we consequently act and behave. In other words, we learn to no longer believe that memories, thoughts, stories and ideas, as they arise in our minds, are themselves real. We develop our mind's capacity to not just 'process' them but to be aware of them as they arise, to observe their impact and how they make us feel. We see their fleeting nature, the way in which a negative mood might influence how our bodies feel, or how we repeat endlessly stories that are not healthy, even a story such as 'I am depressed'. We see how we, unconsciously, habitually judge ourselves negatively and begin to believe and act on these judgements so they become self-fulfilling prophesies.

Williams and Penman put it like this:

[B]y breaking with some of your daily routines you'll progressively dissolve some of these negative thinking patterns and become more mindful and aware. You'll be astonished how much more happiness and joy are attainable with even tiny changes to the way you live your life.[177]

MBCT's cognitive process draws on both *vipassana* and *samatha* (directed and receptive attention) through very specific interventions such as body scans, where we track sensations in our bodies, noticing them without judgement; mindful movement, where we pay very close attention to parts of our physical body as we move; paying attention to the sounds around us to encourage a less reactive and 'decentred' stance in our thinking and learning to become familiar with what we might consider undesirable or difficult thoughts or emotions by looking at them without judgement. The goal is to cultivate a more friendly, kinder attitude towards our selves. We are equipped to choose to move in the direction of nourishment, say, and limit the mental events that drain us or leave us depleted, anxious, irritable in preference for what has been called a 'virtuous cycle' of resilience and greater creativity about life choices.

MBCT thus involves a sophisticated set of tools utilised primarily in clinical settings though not just in one-on-one contexts. I use it illustratively here to point to its distance from Buddhist mindfulness but also to highlight its focus, inevitably perhaps given its therapeutic mode, on individual suffering. All forms of mindfulness, whether in the clinic or the workplace, utilise versions of these tools and share a common language of expanding our choices in the world based on cognitive processes. For critics, this stripped down mindfulness has become a technology of the self. It seeks to change individuals through changing how they think, and carries assumptions about responsibility. Most criticisms of this phenomenon draw on Michel Foucault's concept of biopower, a form of power that marks capitalism's attempt to regulate and control our internal worlds towards greater extraction of value. Biopower sees individuals as economic resources and seeks to control life processes and aptitudes and to correct and manage individual bodies, and according to this view, mindfulness becomes another regulatory mechanism which serves to normalise both privatised stress management and the concept of well-being. In corporate settings, mindfulness enhances the value of employees, increases resilience in the face of change, insecurity or austerity, and increases engagement. In educational settings, it is taught as a way to increase students' personal resourcefulness and to boost performance. In disadvantaged communities, it is about self-regulation towards prescribed desirable behaviour. Those who are the target are stripped of their social and economic contexts to become atomised entities, within which stress or unhappiness is viewed as a failure of the self. Mindfulness extends biopower by situating the causes of stress and suffering within our own reactivity and not in the social, material and economic conditions, and serves to perpetuate the causes and conditions that create our stress and suffering.[178] Thus, *sati*-less mindfulness can be understood as playing the same role in the production of the neoliberal self as therapy culture. In failing to address collective suffering and acknowledge that systemic change is necessary, what we are left with is an endless focus on ourselves: 'a triumph of narcissism'.[179]

Conclusion

What makes the mindfulness industry of particular interest to this book is, of course, that it claims to be originally 'Buddhist' (though sometimes practitioners carefully stress its secular nature) and yet, in its most common iterations, has very little, if anything, to do with Buddhism. Its relationship with Buddhism is therefore complex. I recall a discussion at a seminar in Dublin some years ago where critic of McMindfulness, Terry Hyland – whose work is cited here – led a lively debate during which the case was strongly made that a) all we have is ourselves to work with, and b) even in highly corporatised competitive settings, mindfulness can prove liberatory and, at the very least, lessen the suffering of those working in those settings. These debates are ongoing. My focus in this chapter, however, has been exclusively on the manner in which all of these technologies of self feed into, extend and support the neoliberal self.

Barry Magid, a Zen teacher and psychiatrist, referred to earlier, suggests another way of thinking about this. He argues that the current phenomenon of mindfulness has become steeped in the values of contemporary culture. It has been brought into the technocratic problem-solving world, ever committed to progress and improvement, and there, has become something that is 'used' for specific ends. In contrast, what is unique about spiritual practices such as Buddhist meditation is that they are not meant to be instrumental. Buddhist practitioners are absolutely not engaged in an endless project of refinement, purification or self-improvement, but rather they settle down in meditation to allow awareness of 'things as they already are'.[180]

My interest in reinserting *sati* into how we think about mindfulness is because, as Will Davies argues, the discovery that the source of our happiness is outside of ourselves is deeply liberating.[181] We can be relieved of our sense of guilt and inadequacy when feeling unhappy, and instead fully recognise and act on the fact that we are social beings, that engagement in social or other-orientated actions and activities that allow us participate in a world that is bigger than ourselves is what brings happiness. According to Ron Purser, whose work I have drawn on here, this means that our liberation is found in minute-by-minute meaningful action, guided by a 'conscientious compassion' that celebrates and consolidates our interdependent nature. For contemporary Buddhism, *sati* and the possibility of resisting a deep source of our collective suffering – such as found in neoliberal subjectivity – are not separate.

Conclusion

Twenty years ago philosopher Mary Midgley wrote passionately about the need to cultivate a non-dualistic view of the self in order to deal with the then early-warning stages of climate catastrophe.[182] Her work, still relevant today, points to a fourth 'big idea' that inhabits this book, without quite being named, alongside the other big ideas of neoliberalism, Buddhism and therapy culture. That is, the dualistic vision of the self that first emerged at a particular stage in European history. Often traced to the work of Descartes, dualism divides up things: body from mind, reason from feeling, and humans from the rest of the physical universe. Over time, it has allowed us to divide ourselves up as separate from each other and rationalises our war against nature. This is the self that is pushed to its extremes in the era of neoliberalism and which both circulates in softer tones, and finds solace in therapy culture.

In trying to think critically about this self, and offer an alternative, I chose to reach back to even older ideas, first articulated in a pre-literate social order in rural India, 2,500 years ago. Notwithstanding their adaptation to local cultures and context wherever they landed since, these Buddhist ideas have retained their central core. One such core is the Buddhist account of the self: that our self is irreducibly social, so that we are deeply enmeshed with others and our survival and our happiness depend on how we respond in that enmeshment. We can wreck it, deny it or seek to nurture it. Our freedom is guaranteed not through autonomy from others but through opening ourselves to our mutual constraints and vulnerabilities and exploring these as the shared human experience. It comes from remaining fully and deeply in the world, connected with its many layers of life, sentient and insentient. As we saw, the idea of dependent origination (or the emptiness of self) prompts a particular way of facing the world and suggests a particular set of ethics. Dependent origination says that our flourishing is incompatible with systems that bring forth social, economic and environmental destruction through objectifying and commodifying the earth. When we pollute the seas with tiny microbes of plastic, we eventually poison ourselves. The coronavirus is not separate from our belief in endless 'growth' and its inevitable destruction of biodiversity and ecosystems.

But the good news is that Buddhist ontology makes the case that, even though we are socialised into thinking of ourselves as separate, this dualism can be deconstructed. A powerful contribution of Buddhism to many contemporary issues is its capacity to expose and undermine the mind-fixations that delude us into thinking dualistically. Exposing duality allows us to transform ourselves and change our world.[183] The truth of inter-subjectivity, as a statement of how we are in the world, opens up possibilities for a radically different kind of social and political world. This was the kind of truth that led Tey Sambo to bring kindness to the genocidaire in Cambodia and inspired the Peace and Development Volunteers to continue with their community work in a tense post-conflict environment.

Thus, Buddhism asks us first and foremost to turn inwards, to pay attention to what kind of self we are generating, but to do so in order to turn outwards again, or to do both continuously. In Buddhism, resilience rests in taking a backward step, in letting go of 'self', not building up and solidifying a self. Barry Magid puts its as follows:

> In both zen and psychoanalysis we strive to 'come back' to ourselves, to re-own what has been split off and to embrace what we have warded off. Then we are who we are, each moment is what is. We no longer have to pass our lives through the sieve of approval or disapproval, of 'affirmation and negation'. Life as it is stretches before us 'vast and boundless as outer space'.[184]

This book's purpose, however, is not to suggest that we all need to 'become' Buddhist. Rather, it is to bring our attention to the power of non-self, of emptiness of self, as an antidote to neoliberalism's 'diabolical logic' and as a guide to a path onwards. As a student of Zen, I am encouraged to let go of trying to categorise, sort, define and 'fix' things and to simply allow what is already known be manifest. If I pay very close attention when I sit on my meditation cushion, I will see the emptiness of self manifest itself. As a student of Zen, I am also encouraged to not cling too tightly onto something called 'Zen' or even 'Buddhist' ideas. Zen students quickly get used to the idea that 'not knowing' is a good place from which to start: not knowing means to bracket set views and to be willing to become intimate with whatever is actually going on. This allows us see that the true nature of the self, one's own true nature, lacks nothing. Realising this liberates us to act according to what the situation requires, as we are no longer motivated by the 'misconstrued obsession to become more real'.[185] The truth of intersubjectivity, as a statement of how we are in the world, opens up possibilities for a radically different kind of social and political world. What Buddhism offers is a thoroughgoing, radical account of ontology. It offers us a profound and distinct way of rethinking a politics of life that, unlike neoliberalism's evacuation of the social from the self, says that the social and the self are one. Contemplating the neoliberal self, we can see it is bound tightly without a rope, defensive, isolated and fearful. Buddhism invites us to release ourselves into our true being: expansive, loose, fearless and full of everything and everyone else.

I am moved to conclude by illustrating Zen's contention that its ideas about the social and the self have nothing at all to do with something called 'Buddhism'. They are about the human condition. Hence, I have chosen to end with a poem from someone who, as far as I know, was not Buddhist, and which is about the resolution of a very human impulse to seek revenge through the most complete separation of the self from the other: the killing off of that other. However, as we will see, the poet, Taha Muhammad Ali, takes a backward step and, recognising something true about humanity, comes to a far better conclusion.

Revenge[186]

At times ... I wish
I could meet in a duel
the man who killed my father
and razed our home,
expelling me
into
a narrow country.
And if he killed me,
I'd rest at last,
and if I were ready –
I would take my revenge!

*

But if it came to light,
when my rival appeared,

that he had a mother
waiting for him,
or a father who'd put
his right hand over
the heart's place in his chest
whenever his son was late
even by just a quarter-hour
for a meeting they'd set –
then I would not kill him,
even if I could.

*

Likewise ... I
would not murder him
if it were soon made clear
that he had a brother or sisters
who loved him and constantly longed to see him.
Or if he had a wife to greet him
and children who
couldn't bear his absence
and whom his gifts would thrill.
Or if he had
friends or companions,
neighbours he knew
or allies from prison
or a hospital room,
or classmates from his school ...
asking about him
and sending him regards.

*

But if he turned
out to be on his own –
cut off like a branch from a tree –
without a mother or father,
with neither a brother nor sister,
wifeless, without a child,
and without kin or neighbours or friends,
colleagues or companions,
then I'd add not a thing to his pain
within that aloneness –
not the torment of death,
and not the sorrow of passing away.
Instead I'd be content
to ignore him when I passed him by
on the street – as I
convinced myself
that paying him no attention
in itself was a kind of revenge.

Notes and References

1. Interview on *The Arts Show*, RTE Radio 1, 13 July 2020.

2. B. Evans and J. Reid, 'Exhausted by Resilience: Response to the commentaries', *Resilience: International Politics, Practices and Discourse*, vol. 3, no. 2, 2015, pp. 154–9.

3. See S. Metcalf, 'The Big Idea that Defines Our Era', *The Guardian*, 19 August 2017.

4. W. Brown, *Undoing the Demos: Neoliberalism's stealth revolution* (New York: Zone Books, 2015), pp. 10, 33.

5. B.C. Han, *The Expulsion of the Other* (Cambridge and Medford: Polity Press, 2018).

6. B. Dowds, *Depression and the Erosion of the Self in Late Modernity* (London and New York: Routledge, 2018), p. xv.

7. P. Verhaeghe, *What About Me? The struggle for identity in a market-based society*, 4th edn (Victoria and London: Scribe Publications, 2017), p. 8.

8. N. Rose, *Governing the Soul: The shaping of the private self* (London: Taylor & Francis, 1990).

9. J. McGuigan, 'The Neoliberal Self', *Culture Unbound*, vol. 6, 2014, pp. 223–4.

10. See J. Stiglitz, 'Unfettered Neoliberalism Will Literally Destroy Our Civilization', *Irish Independent*, 7 November 2019.

11. Han, *The Expulsion of the Other*, p. 38.

12. P. Dolan, *Happy Ever After: Escaping the myth of the perfect life* (London: Allen Lane, 2019), p. x.

13. McGuigan, 'The Neoliberal Self', p. 224.

14. I. McGilchrist and R. Rowson, 'Divided Brain, Divided World', in R. Tweedy (ed.), *The Political Self: Understanding the social context for mental illness* (London: Karnac, 2017), pp. 87–9.

15. C. Holland et al., 'Neoliberalism and Education: Spotlight on Ireland', *Policy Futures in Education*, vol. 14, no. 8, 2016, p. 1042.

16. McGuigan, 'The Neoliberal Self', p. 224.

17. L. Scott, *The Four-Dimensional Human: Ways of being in the digital world* (London: Windmill Books, 2015).

18. C. Lavrence and K. Lozanski, 'This Is Not Your Practice Life: Lululemon and the neoliberal governance of self', *Canadian Review of Sociology*, vol. 51, no. 1, 2014, pp. 76–94.

19. Brown, *Undoing the Demos*, p. 37.

20. McGuigan, 'The Neoliberal Self', p. 234.

21. R. Gill, 'Postfeminist Media Culture', *Cultural Studies*, vol. 10, no. 2, 2007, p. 163.

22. Verhaege, *What About Me?*, p. 180.

23. D. Ferraro, 'Notes on Mental Health and Neoliberalism' (2016). Available at melbournelacanian.wordpress.com

24. P. Mason, *Capitalism: A guide to our future* (Milton Keynes: Allen Lane, 2015), p. xi.

25. Verhaeghe, *What About Me?*, p. 77.

26. W. Davies, *The Happiness Industry: How the government and big business sold us well-being* (London and New York: Verso, 2016), p. 145.

27. Two Fuse, *Freedom?* (Síreacht, Cork: Cork University Press, 2018), p. 6.

28. Rose, *Governing the Soul*, p. 171.

29. I. Gershon, 'Neoliberal Agency', *Current Anthropology*, vol. 54, no. 4, 2011, pp. 539–40.

30. B. Ehrenreich, *Natural Causes: Life, death and the illusion of control* (London: Granta, 2018).

31. C. Cederstrom and A. Spicer, *The Wellness Syndrome* (Cambridge and Medford: Polity Press, 2015), p. 22.

32. B. Winegard, 'The Awful Revolution: Is neoliberalism a public health risk?' (2011). Available at: zcomm.org/znetarticle/the-awful-revolution-is-neoliberalism-a-public-health-risk-by-ben-winegard/

33. Rowson and McGilchrist, 'Divided Brain, Divided World', p. 109.

34. J. Reid, 'The Neoliberal Subject: Resilience and the art of living dangerously', *Revista Pléyade*, vol. 10, 2012, pp. 144–65.

35. B. Evans and J. Reid, 'Exhausted by Resilience: Response to the commentaries', *Resilience: International Politics, Practices and Discourse*, vol. 3, no. 2, 2015, p. 154.

36. Cederstrom and Spicer, *The Wellness Syndrome*, p. 133.

37. P. Dardot and C. Laval, 'The New Way of the World. Part 1: Manufacturing the Neoliberal Subject', *E-flux Journal*, vol. 51, no. 1, 2015. Available at: www.e-flux.com/journal/51/59958/the-new-way-of-the-world-part-i-manufacturing-the-neoliberal-subject

38. D. Chandler and J. Reed, *The Neoliberal Subject: Resilience, adaptation and vulnerability* (London: Littlefield & Rowman, 2016).

39. E. Pine, *Notes to Self: Essays* (Dublin: Tramp Press, 2018), p. 179.

40. Brown, *Undoing the Demos*, p. 110.

41. Verhaeghe, *What About Me?*, pp. 214–15.

42. Brown, *Undoing the Demos*, p. 211.

43. Cederstrom and Spicer, *The Wellness Syndrome*, pp. 96, 108.

44. M. Koltai, 'The Neoliberal Self: Some observations on the psychology of contemporary neoliberalism', *LeftEast*, April 2016. Available at: www.criticatac.ro/lefteast/the-neoliberal-self-some-observations-on-the-psychology-of-contemporary-neoliberalism/

45. See *The Irish Times Magazine*, 5 August 2017.

46. Cognitive Behavioural Therapy (CBT) focuses on cognition and seeks to change 'unhelpful' thinking processes and behaviours. See S. Binkey, 'Happiness, Positive Psychology and the Programme of Neoliberal Governmentality,' *Subjectivity*, vol. 4, no. 4, 2011, pp. 371–94; and see Dr Oliver James at www. youtube.com/watch?v=lTgnzee3vFA

47. R. Gill and A.S. Elias, 'Beauty Surveillance: The digital self-monitoring cultures of neoliberalism', *European Journal of Cultural Studies*, vol. 21, no. 1, 2018, pp. 59–77.

48. N. Young, *The Virtual Self: How our digital lives are altering the world around us* (Toronto: McLelland & Stewart, 2012), pp. 28–30.

49. T. Curran and A. Hill, 'Perfectionism Is Increasing over Time: A meta-analysis of birth cohort differences from 1989 to 2016', *Psychological Bulletin*, vol. 145, no. 5, 2017, pp. 410–29.

50. Ibid., p. 414.

51. Ferraro, *Notes on Mental Health*.

52. Davies, *The Happiness Industry*, p. 6.

53. S. Binkey, 'Happiness, Positive Psychology and the Program of Neoliberal Governmentality', *Subjectivity*, vol. 4, no. 4, 2011, p. 384.

54. Ferraro, *Notes on Mental Health*.

55. Davies, *The Happiness Industry*, pp. 4–5.

56. B. Ehrenreich, *Smile or Die: How positive thinking fooled America and the world* (London: Granta, 2009).

57. Davies, *The Happiness Industry*, p. 6.

58. Ibid., p. 250.

59. R. Harris, *The Happiness Trap* (Boston: Trumpeter, 2008), pp. 11–14.

60. Cederstrom and Spicer, *The Wellness Syndrome*, p. 43.

61. Cited in ibid., p. 90.

62. D. Butler, 'Falling Through the Cracks: Precarity, precocity, and other neoliberal pressures', *Fort Da*, vol. 21, no. 2, 2015, pp. 44–6.

63. Reid, 'The Neoliberal Subject', pp. 144–65.

64. Ferraro, *Notes on Mental Health*.

65. Dowds, *Depression and the Erosion of the Self*.

66. O.J. Madsen, 'Therapeutic Culture', in T. Teo (ed.), *Encyclopedia of Critical Psychology* (New York: Springer, 2014), pp. 1965–9.

67. Dowds, *Depression and the Erosion of the Self*, p. xv.

68. See A. Petersen, 'Return of the Age of Anxiety', in K. Keohane et al. (eds), *Late Modern Subjectivity and Its Discontents* (London and New York: Routledge; Taylor & Francis, 2017), p. 31, which makes the case that anxiety disorders such as GAD and social phobia indicate social pathology within the social order.

69. See B. Winegard, *The Awful Revolution*, for data showing that recent economic gains in the US have not produced greater health and happiness.

70. Psychiatrist Jim Lucey on *Today with Sean O'Rourke*, RTÉ Radio 1, 20 March 2019.

71. See www.healthline.com, 'Top 10 Health Conditions Affecting Millennials'.

72. O. James, 'The Good News about Getting Old – Better Mental Health', *Guardian*, 23 July 2010.

73. See Spunout.ie report (2019), 'Young People Are Experiencing More Mental Health Issues than Before'. Available at: https://spunout.ie/news/news/young-people-my-world-survey

74. See www.samaritans.org/ireland/samaritans-ireland/samaritans-ireland-impact-reports/

75. Verhaeghe, *What About Me?*, p. 193.

76. Petersen, 'Return of the Age of Anxiety', p. 35.

77. Dowds, *Depression and the Erosion of the Self*.

78. Verhaeghe, *What About Me?* Verhaeghe's conclusions are drawn from research by both the World Health Organization and the British Psychological Society and he reiterates in his work the latter's warning that, moreover, many diagnostics presented as 'science' derive from social norms rather than biology and are not based on conclusive evidence.

79. Butler, 'Falling Through the Cracks'.

80. Ibid., pp. 33–52.

81. Verhaeghe, *What About Me?*, p. 109.

82. Spunout.ie, 'Young People Are Experiencing More Mental Health Issues than Before'.

83. Verhaeghe, *What About Me?*, p. 248.

84. Two Fuse, *Freedom?*, p. 58.

85. Petersen, 'Return of the Age of Anxiety', p. 38.

86. Dowds, *Depression and the Erosion of the Self*, p. 248.

87. Ibid., pp. xvi–xvii.

88. Butler, 'Falling Though the Cracks', pp. 38–9.

89. Dowds, *Depression and the Erosion of the Self*, p. 180.

90. See Spunout.ie report (2018), 'The Effects of Social Media on Mental Health'. Available at: https://spunout.ie/life/online-wellbeing/social-media-mental-health

91. Verhaeghe, *What About Me?*, p. 193.

92. Ibid., pp. 170–1.

93. Ibid., pp. 134–5.

94. Davies, *The Happiness Industry*, p. 250.

95. Ibid., p. 9.

96. McGuigan, 'The Neoliberal Self'.

97. Davies, *The Happiness Industry*, p. 11.

98. F. Furedi, *Therapy Culture: Cultivating vulnerability in an uncertain age* (London and New York: Routledge, 2004), p. 24.

99. R. Foster, 'The Therapeutic Spirit of Neoliberalism', *Political Theory*, vol. 44, no. 1, 2016, pp. 83–4.

100. Madsen, 'Therapeutic Culture', p. 1965.

101. D.R. Dufour, 'Modern Subjectivity/Post-modern Subjectivity', in K. Keohane et al. (eds), *Late Modern Subjectivity and Its Discontents* (London and New York: Routledge, 2017), pp. 14–16.

102. Foster, 'The Therapeutic Spirit', p. 91.

103. Ibid., p. 86.

104. Rose, *Governing the Soul*.

105. V. Pitts-Taylor, 'The Plastic Brain: Neoliberalism and the neuronal self', *Health*, vol. 14, no. 6, 2010, pp. 635–52.

106. D. Smail, *The Origins of Unhappiness* (Glasgow: Harper Collins, 1993), p. 186.

107. S. Peelo, 'Therapy in the 21st Century: A pimped profession?', *Irish Journal of Counselling and Psychotherapy*, vol. 19, no. 2, 2019, p. 13.

108. H. Jameson, 'The Suffering Artist is a Deadly Myth', *The Irish Times*, 2 February 2019, p. 28.

109. R. Williams, 'Eat, Pray, Love: Producing the female neoliberal spiritual subject', *Journal of Popular Culture*, vol. 47, no. 3, 2011, pp. 613–33.

110. J. Oksala, 'The Neoliberal Subject of Feminism', *Journal of the British Society for Phenomenology*, vol. 42, no. 1, 2011, p. 112.

111. L. Favaro, '"Just Be Confident, Girls": Confidence chic as neoliberal governmentality', in A.S. Elias et al. (eds), *Aesthetic Labour: Rethinking beauty politics in neoliberalism* (London: Palgrave Macmillan, 2017), pp. 283–99.

112. Interview on *The Ryan Tubridy Show*, RTÉ Radio 1, 9 October 2019.

113. See 'Capitalist Realism: An interview with Mark Fisher', by Richard Capes (2011). Available at: http://moretht.blogspot.com/2011/11/capitalist-realism-interview-with-mark.html.

114. N. Makovicky, 'Personhood, Neoliberalism and Postsocialism' (2014). Available at: https://is.muni.cz/el/1423/jaro2018/SAN103/um/makovicky_neolib_personhood_intro_after.pdf.

115. Davies, *The Happiness Industry*, pp. 5–6.

116. D. Smail, 'Understanding the Social Context of Individual Distress', in R. Tweedy (ed.), *The Political Self: Understanding the social context for mental illness* (London: Karnac Books, 2017), pp. 3–28.

117. Verhaeghe, *What About Me?*, p. 182.

118. See J. Watts, 'Our Mental Health Obsession has Fuelled the Politics of Donald Trump and Brexit', *The Independent*, 15 November 2016.

119. Smail, *The Origins of Unhappiness*, p. 20.

120. Chandler and Reed, *The Neoliberal Subject*, p. 170.

121. R. Wilkinson and K. Pickett, *The Spirit Level* (London: Allen Lane, 2009).

122. Cederstrom and Spicer, *The Wellness Syndrome*, p. 134.

123. Han, *The Expulsion of the Other*.

124. R. Smith, *Stepping Out of Self-Deception: The Buddha's liberating teaching of no-self* (Boston and London: Shambala, 2010), p. xii.

125. For instance, Pope John Paul II famously dismissed Buddhism as nihilistic.

126. R. Ricketts, *The Buddha's Radical Psychology: Explorations* (London: Callisto Green, 2016).

127. J. Baggini, *The Ego Trick* (London: Granta, 2011), p. 148.

128. Author's interview with Karen Terzano, Galway, 3 June 2018.

129. Ibid.

130. Author's interview with Pat George, Galway, 3 June 2018.

131. D. Loy, 'Trying to Become Real: A Buddhist critique of some secular heresies', *International Philosophical Quarterly*, vol. 32, no. 4, 1992, pp. 403–25.

132. C. Brazier, *Buddhist Psychology: Liberate your mind, embrace life* (London: Constable & Robinson, 2003), p. 93.

133. Smith, *Stepping Out*, pp. 3–4.

134. A. Olendzki, 'The Transformative Impact of Non-self', in D.K. Nauriyal et al. (eds), *Buddhist Thought and Applied Psychological Research* (London and New York: Routledge, 2010), pp. 252–3. [My italics.]

135. P. Conradi, *Going Buddhist: Panic and emptiness, the Buddha and me* (London: Short Books, 2004), p. 62.

136. Smith, *Stepping Out*, p. 4.

137. K. Jones, *The New Social Face of Buddhism: A call to action* (Boston: Wisdom, 2003), p. 35.

138. Smail, *The Origins of Unhappiness*, pp. 71–5.

139. Jones, *The New Social Face of Buddhism*, p. 37.

140. S.B. King, *Socially Engaged Buddhism* (Honolulu: University of Hawai'i Press, 2009), p. 19.

141. Ibid.

142. B. Kelly, 'Compassion, Cognition and the Illusion of Self: Buddhist notes towards more skilful engagement with diagnostic classification systems in psychiatry', in E. Shonin et al. (eds), *Mindfulness and Buddhist-Derived Approaches in Mental Health and Addiction (Advances in Mental Health and Addiction)* (New York: Springer, 2016), p. 24.

143. See S. Littlefair, 'Leading Neuroscientists and Buddhists Agree: Consciousness is everywhere', *Lions Roar*, 8 January 2017. Available at: https://www.lionsroar.com/christof-koch-unites-buddhist-neuroscience-universal-nature-mind/

144. M. Epstein, *Psychotherapy without the Self: A Buddhist perspective* (New Haven and London: Yale University Press, 2007), p. 11.

145. Olendzki, 'The Transformative Impact of Non-self', p. 255.

146. Author's interview with Brendan Kelly, 3 July 2018.

147. B. Magid, *Ordinary Mind: Exploring the common ground of Zen and psychoanalysis* (Somerville: Wisdom Publications, 2005), p. 24.

148. Author's interview with Brendan Kelly, 3 July 2018.

149. Smith, *Stepping Out*.

150. P. Hershock, *Chan Buddhism* (Honolulu: University of Hawai'i Press, 2005), pp. 137–8.

151. R.S. Ubasak, 'National Political Violence and Buddhism's Response in Cambodia', *Seeds of Peace*, vol. 21, no. 2, 2005, pp. 28–31. *Seeds of Peace* is the publication of the International Network of Engaged Buddhists, edited and published in Bangkok by Sulak Sivaraksa, a leader of this movement.

152. Theravada Buddhism emerged in Southeast Asia: Sri Lanka, Thailand, Cambodia, Myanmar and Laos. Mahayana Buddhism grew from the intermingling of Buddhism with local cultures as it spread to China, Japan, Korea and Tibet. Both traditions have moved westwards and continue to adapt, producing many varieties of Buddhism today worldwide. The remainder of this section, on the Cambodian historical context, comes from I. Harris, *Cambodian Buddhism: History and practice* (Honolulu: University of Hawai'i Press, 2005).

153. Cited in ibid., p. 145. Sihanouk reigned twice: 1941–55 (during which time he oversaw Cambodia's independence from France) and 1993–2004.

154. Harris, *Cambodian Buddhism*, pp. 183–5.

155. All interviews cited here were conducted by me in Cambodia between 17 and 27 March 2008.

156. King, *Socially Engaged Buddhism*, p. 39.

157. Ibid., pp. 53–4.

158. Ibid., p. 56.

159. B. Victoria, *Zen War Stories* (Abingdon: Routledge, 2002).

160. See H. Beach, 'It Is Our Duty: The rise of militant aggression in Buddhism', *Irish Times*, 11 July 2019.

161. See E. Copley, 'Out of Order', *South China Morning Post*, 13 March 2008.

162. S.J. Tambiah, *Buddhism Betrayed? Religion, politics and violence in Sri Lanka* (Chicago and London: University of Chicago Press, 1992), pp. 102–28.

163. An advertorial selling mindfulness workshops offered better sex as one of its five 'surprising perks'. *Irish Times Magazine*, 13 June 2020.

164. T. Hyland, 'McMindfulness in the Workplace: Vocational learning and the commodification of the present moment', *Journal of Vocational Education and Training*, vol. 67, no. 2, 2015, pp. 219–34.

165. See M. Richtel, 'The Latest in Military Strategy: Mindfulness', *New York Times*, 5 April 2019, for the use of mindfulness with US forces in Iraq and in US military generally, and in UK and New Zealand military training.

166. Cited in Jones, *The New Social Face of Buddhism*, p. 101.

167. Hyland, 'McMindfulness in the Workplace', p. 229.

168. 'McMindfulness' means a standardised set of interventions, utilised franchise-style, following the manner of McDonald's restaurants.

169. R. Purser, *McMindfulness: How mindfulness became the new capitalist spirituality* (London: Repeater, 2019), pp. 10–11.

170. N. Fischer, *The World Could Be Otherwise: Imagination and the Bodhisattva path* (Boulder: Shambala, 2019), p. 10.

171. Thanks to Ryoshin Paul Haller for this terminology.

172. S. Batchelor, *Confessions of a Buddhist Atheist* (New York: Spiegel & Grau, 2010), pp. 25–6.

173. Fischer, *The World Could Be Otherwise*, pp. 142–3.

174. Purser, *McMindfulness*.

175. See D. Forbes, 'How Capitalism Captured the Mindfulness Industry', *Guardian*, 16 April 2019.

176. M. Williams and D. Penman, *Mindfulness: A practical guide to finding peace in a frantic world* (London: Piatkus, 2011), pp. 2–3.

177. Ibid., p. 13.

178. Z. Walsh. 'Mindfulness under Neoliberal Governmentality', *Journal of Management, Spirituality and Religion*, vol. 15, no. 2, 2018, pp. 109–22.

179. Purser, *McMindfulness*, p. 242.

180. An interview with Barry Magid and Robert Rosenblum, The Garrison Institute, New York, 2016. Available at https://www.garrisoninstitute.org/blog/whats-wrong-with-mindfulness/

181. Davies, *The Happiness Industry*, pp. 246–76.

182. M. Midgley, 'Individualism and the Concept of Gaia', *Review of International Studies*, vol. 26, 2006, pp. 29–44.

183. D. Loy, *The Great Awakening: A Buddhist social theory* (Somerville: Wisdom Publications, 2003), p. 196.

184. Magid, *Ordinary Mind*, p. 177.

185. D. Loy, *Ecodharma: Buddhist teachings for the ecological crisis* (Somerville: Wisdom Publications, 2018), p. 68.

186. Taha Muhammad Ali, 'Revenge', in *So What: New & selected poems 1971–2005* (Port Townsend, WA: Copper Canyon Press, 2006).

Bibliography

Baggini, J., *The Ego Trick* (London: Granta, 2011)

Batchelor, S., *Confession of a Buddhist Atheist* (New York: Spiegel & Grau, 2010)

Binkey, S., 'Happiness, Positive Psychology and the Programme of Neoliberal Governmentality', *Subjectivity*, vol. 4, no. 4, 2011, pp. 371–94

Brazier, C., *Buddhist Psychology: Liberate your mind, embrace life* (London: Constable & Robinson, 2003)

Brown, W., *Undoing the Demos: Neoliberalism's stealth revolution* (New York: Zone Books, 2015)

Butler, D., 'Falling Through the Cracks: Precarity, precocity, and other neoliberal pressures', *Fort Da*, vol. 21, no. 2, 2015, pp. 33–52

Cederstrom, C. and A. Spicer, *The Wellness Syndrome* (Cambridge and Medford: Polity Press, 2015)

Chandler, D. and J. Reed, *The Neoliberal Subject: Resilience, adaptation and vulnerability* (London: Rowman & Littlefield, 2016)

Conradi, P., *Going Buddhist: Panic and emptiness, the Buddha and me* (London: Short Books, 2004)

Curran, T. and A. Hill, 'Perfectionism Is Increasing over Time: A meta-analysis of birth cohort differences from 1989 to 2016', *Psychological Bulletin*, vol. 145, no. 5, 2017, pp. 410–29

Dardot, P. and C. Laval, 'The New Way of the World. Part 1: Manufacturing the Neoliberal Subject, *E-flux Journal*, vol. 51, no. 1, 2015. Available at: www.e-flux.com/journal/51/59958/the-new-way-of-the-world-part-i-manufacturing-the-neoliberal-subject

Davies, W., *The Happiness Industry: How the government and big business sold us well-being* (London and New York: Verso, 2016)

Dolan, P., *Happy Ever After: Escaping the myth of the perfect life* (London: Allen Lane, 2019)

Dowds, B., *Depression and the Erosion of the Self in Late Modernity* (London and New York: Routledge, 2018)

Dufour, D.R., 'Modern Subjectivity/Post-modern Subjectivity', in K. Keohane et al. (eds), *Late Modern Subjectivity and Its Discontents* (London and New York: Routledge, 2017), pp. 8–23

Ehrenreich B., *Smile or Die: How positive thinking fooled America and the world* (London: Granta, 2009)

Ehrenreich, B., *Natural Causes: Life, death and the illusion of control* (London: Granta, 2018)

Epstein, M., *Psychotherapy without the Self: A Buddhist perspective* (New Haven and London: Yale University Press, 2007)

Evans, B. and J. Reid, 'Exhausted by Resilience: Response to the commentaries', *Resilience: International Politics, Practices and Discourse*, vol. 3, no. 2, 2015, pp. 154–9

Favaro, L., '"Just Be Confident, Girls": Confidence chic as neoliberal governmentality', in A.S. Elias, R. Gill and C.M. Scharff (eds), *Aesthetic Labour: Rethinking beauty politics in neoliberalism* (London: Palgrave Macmillan, 2017), pp. 283–99

Ferraro, D., 'Notes on Mental Health and Neoliberalism' (2016). Available at melbournelacanian.wordpress.com

Fischer, N., *The World Could Be Otherwise: Imagination and the Bodhisattva path* (Boulder: Shambala, 2019)

Foster, R., 'The Therapeutic Spirit of Neoliberalism', *Political Theory*, vol. 44, no. 1, 2016, pp. 83–4

Furedi, F., *Therapy Culture: Cultivating vulnerability in an uncertain age* (London and New York: Routledge, 2004)

Gershon, I., 'Neoliberal Agency', *Current Anthropology*, vol. 54, no. 4, 2011, pp. 537–55

Gill, R., 'Postfeminist Media Culture', *Cultural Studies*, vol. 10, no. 2, 2007, pp. 147–66

Gill, R. and A.S. Elias, 'Beauty Surveillance: The digital self-monitoring cultures of neoliberalism', *European Journal of Cultural Studies*, vol. 21, no. 1, 2018, pp. 59–77

Han, B.C., *The Expulsion of the Other* (Cambridge and Medford: Polity Press, 2018)

Harris, I., *Cambodian Buddhism: History and practice* (Honolulu: University of Hawai'i Press, 2005)

Harris, R., *The Happiness Trap: How to stop struggling and start living* (Boston: Trumpeter, 2008)

Hershock, P., *Chan Buddhism* (Honolulu: University of Hawai'i Press, 2005)

Holland, C., et al., 'Neoliberalism and Education: Spotlight on Ireland', *Policy Futures in Education*, vol. 14, no. 8, 2016, pp. 1041–5

Hyland, T., 'McMindfulness in the Workplace: Vocational learning and the commodification of the present moment', *Journal of Vocational Education and Training*, vol. 67, no. 2, 2015, pp. 219–34

Jones, K., *The New Social Face of Buddhism: A call to action* (Boston: Wisdom, 2003)

Kelly, B., 'Compassion, Cognition and the Illusion of Self: Buddhist notes towards more skilful engagement with diagnostic classification systems in psychiatry', in E. Shonin et al. (eds), *Mindfulness and Buddhist-Derived Approaches in Mental Health and Addiction (Advances in Mental Health and Addiction)* (New York: Springer, 2016), pp. 9–28

Keohane, K., et al, 'Introduction to a Series', in K. Keohane et al. (eds), *Late Modern Subjectivity and Its Discontents* (London and New York: Routledge; Taylor & Francis, 2017), pp. 1–7

King, S.B., *Socially Engaged Buddhism* (Honolulu: University of Hawai'i Press, 2009)

Koltai, M., 'The Neoliberal Self: Some observations on the psychology of contemporary neoliberalism', *LeftEast*, April 2016. Available at: www.criticatac.ro/lefteast/the-neoliberal-self-some-observations-on-the-psychology-of-contemporary-neoliberalism/

Lavrence, C. and K. Lozanski, 'This Is Not Your Life Practice: Lululemon and the neoliberal governance of self', *Canadian Review of Sociology*, vol. 51, no. 1, 2014, pp. 76–94

Littlefair, S., 'Leading Neuroscientists and Buddhists Agree: Consciousness is everywhere', *Lions Roar*, 8 January 2017. Available at: https://www.lionsroar.com/christof-koch-unites-buddhist-neuroscience-universal-nature-mind/

Loy, D., 'Trying to Become Real: A Buddhist critique of some secular heresies', *International Philosophical Quarterly*, vol. 32, no. 4, 1992, pp. 403–25

Loy, D., *The Great Awakening: A Buddhist social theory* (Somerville: Wisdom Publications, 2003)

Loy, D., *Ecodharma: Buddhist teachings for the ecological crisis* (Somerville: Wisdom Publications, 2018)

Madsen, O.J., 'Therapeutic Culture', in T. Teo (ed.), *Encyclopedia of Critical Psychology* (New York: Springer, 2014), pp. 1965–9

Magid, B., *Ordinary Mind: Exploring the common ground of Zen and psychoanalysis* (Somerville: Wisdom Publications, 2005)

Mason, P., *Capitalism: A guide to our future* (Milton Keynes: Allen Lane, 2015)

McGuigan, J., 'The Neoliberal Self', *Culture Unbound*, vol. 6, 2014, pp. 223–40

Midgley, M., 'Individualism and the Concept of Gaia', *Review of International Studies*, vol. 26, 2006, pp. 29–44

Oksala, J., 'The Neoliberal Subject of Feminism', *Journal of the British Society for Phenomenology*, vol. 42, no. 1, 2011, pp. 104–20

Olendzki, A., 'The Transformative Impact of Non-self', in D.K. Nauriyal et al. (eds), *Buddhist Thought and Applied Psychological Research* (London and New York: Routledge, 2010), pp. 250–61

Peelo. S., 'Therapy in the 21st Century: A pimped profession?', *Irish Journal of Counselling and Psychotherapy*, vol. 19, no. 2, 2019, pp. 13–16

Petersen, A., 'Return of the Age of Anxiety', in K. Keohane et al. (eds), *Late Modern Subjectivity and Its Discontents* (London and New York: Routledge, 2017), pp. 24–40

Pine, E., *Notes to Self: Essays* (Dublin: Tramp Press, 2018)

Pitts-Taylor, V., 'The Plastic Brain: Neoliberalism and the neuronal self', *Health*, vol. 14, no. 6, 2010, pp. 635–52

Purser, R., *McMindfulness: How mindfulness became the new capitalist spirituality* (London: Repeater, 2019)

Reid, J., 'The Neoliberal Subject: Resilience and the art of living dangerously', *Revista Pléyade*, vol. 10, 2012, pp. 144–65

Ricketts. R., *The Buddha's Radical Psychology: Explorations* (London: Callisto Green, 2016)

Rose, N., *Governing the Soul: The shaping of the private self* (London: Taylor & Francis, 1990)

Rowson, J. and I. McGilchrist, 'Divided Brain, Divided World', in R. Tweedy (ed.), *The Political Self: Understanding the social context for mental illness* (London: Karnac, 2017), pp. 87–113

Scott, L., *The Four-Dimensional Human: Ways of being in the digital world* (London: Windmill Books, 2015)

Smail, D., *The Origins of Unhappiness* (Glasgow: Harper Collins, 1993)

Smail, D., 'Understanding the Social Context of Individual Distress', in R. Tweedy (ed.), *The Political Self: Understanding the social context for mental illness* (London: Karnac Books, 2017), pp. 3–28

Smith R., *Stepping Out of Self-Deception: The Buddha's liberating teaching of no-self* (Boston and London: Shambala, 2010)

Tambiah, S.J., *Buddhism Betrayed? Religion, politics and violence in Sri Lanka* (Chicago and London: University of Chicago Press, 1992)

Two Fuse, *Freedom?* (Síreacht, Cork: Cork University Press, 2018)

Ubasak, R.S., 'National Political Violence and Buddhism's Response in Cambodia', *Seeds of Peace*, vol. 21, no. 2, 2005, pp. 28–31

Verhaege, P., *What About Me? The struggle for identity in a market-based society* (Victoria and London: Scribe Publications, 2017)

Victoria, B., *Zen War Stories* (Abingdon: Routledge, 2002)

Walsh, Z., 'Mindfulness under Neoliberal Governmentality', *Journal of Management, Spirituality and Religion*, vol. 15, no. 2, 2018, pp. 109–22

Wilkinson, R. and K. Pickett, *The Spirit Level* (London: Allen Lane, 2009)

Williams, M. and D. Penman, *Mindfulness: A practical guide to finding peace in a frantic world* (London: Piatkus, 2011)

Williams, R., 'Eat, Pray, Love: Producing the female neoliberal spiritual subject', *Journal of Popular Culture*, vol. 47, no. 3, 2011, pp. 613–33

Winegard, B., 'The Awful Revolution: Is neoliberalism a public health risk?' (2011). Available at: zcomm.org/znetarticle/the-awful-revolution-is-neoliberalism-a-public-health-risk-by-ben-winegard/

Index